D

API

THE MORE-THAN-JUST-SURVIVING HANDBOOK

BARBARA LAW
MARY ECKES

THE MORE-THAN-JUST-SURVIVING HANDBOOK

ESL FOR EVERY CLASSROOM TEACHER

PEGUIS PUBLISHERS
WINNIPEG   CANADA

Printed and bound in Canada

93   94   95   5   4

Canadian Cataloguing in Publication Data

Law, Barbara, 1950–

The more-than-just-surviving handbook: ESL for every classroom teacher

ISBN   0-920541-98-4

1. English language – Study and teaching as a second language*. I. Eckes, Mary, 1954–. II. Title.

PE1128.A2L28   1990   428/.007   C90-097169-X

Book and cover design: Laura Ayers
Illustrations: Scott Barham

Peguis Publishers Limited
520 Hargrave Street
Winnipeg MB Canada   R3A 0X8

CONTENTS

INTRODUCTION

1. FIRST DAYS

2. TESTING AND PLACEMENT

3. LANGUAGE LEARNING—STUDENTS AND TEACHERS

4. WHOLE LANGUAGE LEARNING AND THE FOUR SKILLS

5. READING

6. *WRITING*

7. SPEAKING AND LISTENING

8. CONTENT AREA INSTRUCTION

9. RESOURCES

CONCLUSION

ACKNOWLEDGMENTS

More Than Just Surviving is a book about something we care deeply about—people from other lands and cultures who are struggling to learn our language, and the teachers who are trying to help them. We are grateful to those who have helped us in the writing of this book.

Our thanks go: to Judy Norget, our editor; to Mary Blocksma for her criticisms of the first drafts of this work; to Betsy Metzger who helped shape the initial ideas; to Ellen Simon and Trent Copland for their contributions on the use of computers and interpreters with ESL students; to Kay Ferrell for allowing us to pick her brains time and time again; to our cars for seldom failing during the long drives up and down the mountains. But mostly we thank our families, John, Jeremy, and Elise, and Ken, Katie, and Nicholas, for their unflagging love and support; their tolerance during the endless phone calls, the hours at the computer, and the days spent away from home; and, above all, for their belief that we could do it.

EDITOR'S NOTE   *One of the dilemmas facing today's editor is that of retaining writing clarity while ensuring gender balance. This relates specifically to the use of the personal pronouns **he/she**, **him/her**, **himself/herself**, and so on. Using both forms in all cases makes for particularly awkward reading. In this book, we have chosen to use masculine pronouns in references to ESL students, but we assure the reader that no affront is intended in any way.*

INTRODUCTION

It can be a daunting prospect to be faced with a student who can speak no English. It might make you feel helpless, maybe even resentful. When a new student such as Chan enters the classroom you ask yourself: What can I do with this student? How can I teach him anything if he is not able to understand even the simplest words in English? How can I, who can't speak a word of his language, communicate with him? What can I best do to help him become a member of this class? Many times our first impulse is to panic and say, "Send him to someone else—*anyone!*—who knows what to do."

But resources are not always available. There may not be anyone in your district who can speak your student's language. There might not be an ESL specialist available. Even if your school or district *has* an ESL teacher, he or she may be able to spare only two half-hour sessions a week for your student. Or your student may be getting ESL help, but may already have been mainstreamed into your science, math, or social studies class. Ready or not, he is there.

Many books have been written for ESL teachers but these almost always presuppose a working knowledge of second-language theory, methods, and techniques—and that the teacher is working solely with ESL students. For regular classroom teachers these books are not helpful. You may have twenty-five students, fifteen native-English speakers, the rest non-English speakers. This means that you must meet the needs of many types and levels of students— your regular students who can understand the language and keep up with the mandated curriculum, and your ESL students, who may or may not have any English at all, who may or may not know how to read. Being successful with this range of students requires a totally different set of strategies.

Chapter Overview

This book has been written for those of you who are regular classroom teachers, both elementary and secondary, to give you a place to start, and enough knowledge and strategies to help you cope and to help your ESL students learn. There *are* things you can do, using the resources you have in the classroom and the community to help. **In this book we have undertaken to**

❑ **Distill the latest research on first and second language learning, literacy theory, and integrating the skills of reading, writing, speaking, and listening**

❑ **Apply the latest research to the regular classroom that contains both native-English speakers and non-English-speaking students**

❑ **Suggest activities to foster language acquisition within the context of the regular curriculum**

The activities and methods we suggest have been selected because they are appropriate for both English-speaking and ESL students.

Chapter 1, "First Days," discusses strategies for coping and for helping your ESL students get acquainted with school and classmates. Suggestions are made regarding immediate activities to occupy these students until they can pick up enough English to function as regular students.

This chapter also discusses priorities—things they must know first—as well as how to set short- and long-term goals.

Chapter 2, "Testing and Placement," is of special interest to principals and counselors, as well as classroom teachers. We address the issues of placing the student in the most appropriate grade; measuring reading, writing, speaking, and listening fluency; strategies for grading.

Chapter 3, "Language Learning—Students and Teachers," discusses the principles of second-language learning; the factors that affect the success of the learner; what the teacher can do to promote success; and behavior—how to understand and assist your student when his behavior is inappropriate.

Chapter 4, "Whole Language Learning and the Four Skills," deals with basic literacy, integrating whole language teaching strategies and learning, in every class from English to math.

Chapters 5, 6, and 7—"Reading," "Writing," and "Speaking and Listening," discuss in detail these four skills. We answer frequently asked questions, give suggestions for teaching, and show when and how to correct errors.

Chapter 8, "Content Area Instruction," is written specifically for content teachers. We show how to modify lessons so that students who are not fully fluent in English can succeed in content area classes.

Chapter 9, "Resources," discusses the most effective use of aides, and how to tap the resources of school and community.

Recurrent Themes, Critical for Maximizing Learning

There are several recurrent themes that we believe are critical for maximizing learning.

Language is learned best when the learner feels safe. The kind of atmosphere that pervades your classroom can make the difference between silent non-learners and eager learners:

THE CLASSROOM ENVIRONMENT

❑ A classroom where all students are wanted and respected for themselves and for the contributions they can make

❑ A classroom that is as stress-free as possible, where students can feel free to attempt to use their new language without fear of correction, ridicule, or punishment

❑ A classroom that validates the students' experiences and uses them for learning purposes

Language is learned best when it is "whole" and in context. The focus in the whole language approach is on meaning in language, using language to communicate. In whole language, the four skills of reading, writing, speaking, and listening are parts of a whole, and all four skills are essential components of each activity. Reading does not occur in isolation but is extended to include discussion and writing; composing does not take place without a great deal of prior discussion and reading. And opportunities to learn the language arts are not limited to language arts classes, but are integrated across the curriculum to include content classes too.

USING THE WHOLE LANGUAGE APPROACH

Whole language also means that, instead of concentrating on component parts—the alphabet and phonics before learning to read; vocabulary, then sentences, then paragraphs before learning to write; grammar and the correct pronunciation of English words before being allowed to engage in conversation—students learn to read and write by reading and writing whole stories and texts, to speak by jumping into conversations regardless of whether or not their English is correct and complete.

Whole language means that all teaching/learning activities have meaning and purpose. This means finding things out because the answers have real practical value, or writing well because the work is going to be shared with others.

Whole language also means the teacher has faith in the learners and sets high expectations for them, whatever their literacy level or competence in English.

Whole language recognizes that there is no "right" age or sequence of learning the strands of language, but that there is "a continuum of learning" on which students learn according to their own individual stage of development.

THE IMPORTANCE OF MODELS

Language is learned best when the student is surrounded by real language used for real purposes by real people. Being exposed to the language and having good models are both essential to becoming competent readers, writers, and speakers in that language. The classroom should be set up so that communication in the new language is essential to your ESL students, and so that they are not ignored and forgotten because they have not yet mastered the intricacies of the English language.

ERRORS ARE JUST A PART OF LEARNING

Language is learned best when errors are viewed in their proper perspective, as just a normal part of learning. Any attempt to master a skill, whether skiing, riding a skateboard, writing, or learning another language, involves trial and error during the course of practice. Many of us who took a foreign language in high school or college learned the hard way that errors were viewed as faults, as graphic demonstrations that something was not learned. Errors were punished and eradicated. Perfection was the goal, whether in grammar, pronunciation, reading aloud, or writing.

Research now shows that errors should be viewed as stages in the learner's progression toward competent reading, writing, or speaking in the new language. Learners start with the big issues, such as getting their thoughts articulated and their needs met. Gradually they sort out the details—the correct tenses, the word order, the right words—refining and honing their knowledge of the language. This doesn't happen overnight; it is a long slow process. Recognizing learning as a process, and errors as a natural phenomenon, involves an entirely different attitude toward errors. They are not signs of incompetence or faulty learning, only that something has not yet been learned; therefore, they are not to be pounced on and "fixed" immediately, but considered as indicators of progress, to be noted and tolerated.

Why We Have Written This Book

We have written this book in the hopes that the reader, knowing something about language acquisition and equipped with the knowledge that good teaching is good teaching, whether to English or non-English speakers, will feel empowered, and will be able to accept and welcome all comers to the classroom.

We have included many of our own experiences in the form of anecdotes and brief character sketches in order to make the theory more concrete and the text more real. We have found, as instructors and colleagues over the years, that once a person becomes involved with teaching ESL, it not only becomes an interest, it becomes a passion. We have found working with newcomers to be deeply satisfying, and that the rewards of teaching non-English speakers far outweigh the stumblings and the frustrations. We hope that through this book we can pass on some of our passion and make life a little easier for those in the trenches.

A Word About Labels

There are many different labels for non-English speaking students: ESL, LEP, LES, NEP. None of these are very satisfactory.

ESL, English as a Second Language, is somewhat misleading because many of our students arrive with English as their third, fourth, or even fifth language. In addition, not all ESL students have poor skills in English or require the services of a trained professional. Their reading is often on par with our English-speaking students, and their knowledge of grammar is sometimes even better, although their spoken English may be a little difficult to understand. LEP, Limited English Proficiency, LES, Limited English Speaking, and NES, Non-English Speaking, all carry negative connotations, as if the students arrive with a deficit, needing instruction to fill the gap. In truth, they arrive with a perfectly good language of their own, in which they are fluent, able  to think and speak their needs with ease. They have simply been placed in a situation where the language they have is not the language they need to function in the schools and larger society.

In this book we have chosen to use the most commonly used term, ESL, referring to those students whose first language is other than English, and whose proficiency is not high enough to perform equally with their English-speaking peers. We use this term simply because it is the best known and most commonly understood of all the prevailing labels. Some professionals are currently pushing the label PEP, Potentially English Proficient, but this has not caught on, and we feel it is similar to other euphemistic labels that only sugar-coat the reality. Fiddling with the label does not necessarily change the perception toward the person wearing it.

FIRST DAYS

1

This chapter deals with the arrival of the new ESL student and provides strategies to help the teacher cope. We will focus on

- Preparing for the arrival of the new student
- Familiarizing the new student with school and classroom routines
- Utilizing school and community resources for support in working with the new student
- Teaching strategies for the first days
- Setting up short- and long-range goals for the year

The first day an ESL student comes to class is often traumatic for the teacher, the new student, and the rest of the class. At best, the teacher feels awkward and apprehensive; at worst, terrified and helpless. As teachers, we're used to having some degree of control, but nothing erodes that confidence faster than an inability to communicate with someone.

Feelings of apprehension and nervousness are natural. It is a truly intimidating prospect to be faced with the responsibility of teaching a student—or a group of students—with whom you are unable to communicate. It's only human to feel a wave of panic when that non-English-speaking student is first brought to your classroom. However, when you realize that this apprehension is only a fraction of what the new student is experiencing, it becomes a little easier to get past that first gut-level reaction of, "Oh no, why my class?" and begin coming up with strategies

"My first class in the School"

My first day in class, I take the bus, I filing
scared, I don't have any friends
only the teachers, in one class i dont
have work, i feel stupid in the
others classes i have work, in the
classes i am stupid because I don't
understant something, in the second day
in ~~the~~ class i craying becas
she say in the library you take
one book and I dont noo what book
in the others month's I feel right

to turn the situation into a positive one—for you, the new student, and the rest of your class.

What To Do First

In an ideal situation, students will come to school with their parents to register, and then return the following day, or after they have taken care of such necessities as immunizations and validation of immigration papers. This gives you some preparation time. In reality, students frequently arrive one morning, with no notice (and often after the school year has begun), leaving the two of you to make the best of things. Let's say that Bounkham, a young Laotian, has been assigned to your classroom. With or without lead time, some very important first steps must be taken to establish a relationship.

ESTABLISH A RELATIONSHIP

- **Sensitize the class.** If you've been alerted beforehand, try to learn as much about Bounkham as you can *before* he comes to class so that you can share this information with the other students. This will help them accept Bounkham and make him part of the class. Have the class brainstorm or discuss how it might feel to be immersed into a new country or in the case of Native Americans, a new environment, where they don't speak, read, write, or understand the language.

- **Make the student feel welcome.** Even if you don't know a single word of Bounkham's language, you can show encouragement, sincerity, and empathy through your gestures and body language. Smiling is universal.

- **Make sure you know how to pronounce and spell the student's name.** If you can't figure out the pronunciation of Bounkham's name from the intake form, ask him. Don't try to anglicize his name unless his parents have expressed this wish or he has changed it himself. Calling Bounkham "Bob" could make him feel even more alienated, as if his given name was not good enough. Identity is intricately tied to one's name, and to change it, either in the mistaken belief that the change will make him feel more part of the group or because his name is difficult to pronounce, can damage his integrity and feelings of self-worth.

- **Introduce the student to the class.** Use a map to show the class where Bounkham is from. He may be able to point out his country and tell the class a little about it.

- **If possible, learn a few words and phrases in the student's native language**, such basics as "Hello," "How are you?" and, "Do you understand?" Even a simple thing such as "Hello" (in his language) will make him prick up his ears and brighten up, as well as convey that you are sincere and caring.

- **Be a model of respect for the other students in the class.** People of all ages can be cruel, especially when they don't understand another person's culture or dress. Showing respect for one's right to wear a turban, braids, or clothes we consider garish sets the parameters for appropriate behavior toward the new student, no matter how different he may be.

At the elementary level

- **Give your new student a name tag,** but make sure all the other children in the class have name tags too. Wearing the only name tag in the room can make a child feel alienated and singled out. Making name tags is a perfect classroom activity to get the newcomer and the rest of the class involved in learning each other's names.

  You might consider including Bounkham's parents' name, address, and phone number on the reverse side—information that would be invaluable should he become lost on the way to or from school. But use your own discretion in providing name tags that include students' addresses and phone numbers. In a dangerous part of town, having such a label on a small person could lead to trouble. However, name tags with information on them may be preferable to a child wandering aimlessly about unfamiliar streets, unable to ask for help.

- **Take Polaroid photographs of each student in your class, then use these to make a wall chart according to the seating arrangement of the classroom.** This will reinforce the matching of names with faces.

At the secondary level

- **Always introduce your new student to the class using the correct pronunciation of his name.** High schoolers particularly can wreak havoc with an unfamiliar one. If you can, supplement this introduction with some discussion of the geography and culture of his country.

- **For the first days, ask for a class volunteer willing to help the new student with classroom procedures.** For example, this volunteer may help the new student with the routine for starting class, helping with such basics as providing the new student with paper and a pencil, sharpening the pencil, finding and using classroom resource materials, and so on. This volunteer student may also demonstrate any special activities or equipment you have in your classroom, such things as a computer game, a tape player and music, or reading tapes.

Sometimes a group of students will pitch in and help out. So much of what happens depends on the class makeup and the ESL student's personality. If Bounkham is outgoing and has some English, chances are that other students will help him get acquainted, with no prompting from you. But if Bounkham has no background in English and a shy personality, accept the fact that it will take time for him to join in actively. Try to encourage volunteers to help out. As you see Bounkham relax, include him in small-group activities, ones that include the volunteers who have helped him. Your objective is to move Bounkham from interacting only with individuals, to a small group, and finally to the whole class.

- **Use an introductory small-group activity for junior high or high school students**; for example, create a bulletin board of favorite pictures or photos that your students bring in and label. Then, in small groups, have the students share why they chose to bring in the picture they did. Bounkham will be exposed to different hobbies, pastimes, and so on, and will be able to associate the new faces he sees with activities that may interest him. This can be especially helpful when the new student is trying to get to know classmates who don't sit in the same seats every day.

Learning the School and Its Routines

Your first priority is getting Bounkham used to the layout of the school and the daily routines, and teaching him some basic survival phrases. Because many students have never been in a school before, or because their country's school system is radically different from ours, assume they know nothing. As quickly as possible, acquaint Bounkham with his new school and community. It is also important that parents are given some basic information about the school. In Appendix A we provide a sample information letter to parents. (If parents are not sufficiently literate in English, this may need to be translated.)

The average school day, with the routines and transitions we take for granted, can be perilous for a non-English speaker. One tense afternoon at a junior high school where Barb worked, a new student boarded the first bus that passed, a bus which went downtown instead of to her housing project. Gaida rode the bus for two hours while her parents and teachers waited anxiously, not knowing where she had gone.

One can only guess how many times a student has faithfully come to school in the morning only to find the school deserted and the doors locked, because neither the student nor his parents understood it was to be a holiday, or, worse, could not read the bulletins and had no one to translate. High school ESL students are further handicapped because many announcements about the school's frequently changing routine (i.e., assembly schedule, half-day teacher meetings, and so on) are made over a public address system. The English-language learner must struggle to understand the content of these messages with no visual cues, and because of this often fails to understand. An alert homeroom teacher would write important announcements on the board so that literate ESL students could read the messages as well as hear them. When notices are sent home, schools with available resources might consider having school communications translated into the ESL students' native tongues, or enlisting the assistance of community interpreters to ensure the messages are received.

The teacher can help ease the adjustment period by providing some sort of orientation. One school in northern California has put together a videotape, translated into Hmong and Spanish. Even though few of the parents own a VCR, many own TVs and either rent a VCR or gather at the home of someone who has one. They are then able to learn the routines and regulations on their own time, discussing among themselves those things that need clarification.

THINGS YOUR STUDENT NEEDS TO KNOW

- **How to find the washrooms** (and how to tell which ones are for which gender).

- **How to find his way around the school**: the location of the playground, the cafeteria, gym, his classes. And if Bounkham is in junior high or high school, he will need to find his way from one class to another in the allotted time. He will also need to know the amount of time given for nutrition or morning break and lunch.

- **How to find the main office, the nurse's office, the counselor's office, and so on.** Bounkham needs to know where to bring late/tardy slips, where to go if he doesn't feel well, and so on.

- **How to find the way back to his class from any of these places.** (It might help to write your room number on a card for Bounkham to carry if he leaves your room for anything; in a new place, all doors and even all teachers can look alike.)

HOW TO GET AROUND IN SCHOOL

- **The names of a few key people, especially yours.** In many cultures it is a sign of respect to call a teacher "Teacher," but time and time again, teachers have been dismayed that, after months of being in school, the student still does not know their names.

- **How to open and close his locker**, particularly if it has a lock with a combination.

- **The mechanics of the school day**
  - When must Bounkham arrive?
  - When are recess periods or breaks?
  - When are lunch periods?
  - When is the school day over?
  - What are the dates of vacations and holidays?

- **School rules**
  - What if he's going to be absent or late? Do his parents need to let the school know ahead of time?
  - Does he need to bring in a written excuse for an absence?
  - In secondary schools, are there absent slips that all the teachers must sign and then turn in at the end of the day? Where do these slips need to be returned?

- **Expectations of behavior at school**
  - How is Bounkham supposed to address you?
  - Does he need to raise his hand to be acknowledged?
  - Does he need to stand by his seat, as many cultures demand, when it is his turn to speak?
  - Is talking allowed when working in small groups?
  - Is cooperative work allowed or is Bounkham expected to work on his own? (Mary had a student who was constantly admonished for cheating in his content classes. When a meeting was held with Ming and his teachers, they discovered that he had no idea that working on a paper with another student was wrong. At the school he attended in his homeland they always worked on the answers together.)
  - What is the school's policy and procedure for detentions?
  - If Bounkham has a detention after school for misbehavior, where is he to go and for how long?
  - What is he expected to do during detention? (With regard to detentions or other emergency situations when the parents need to be contacted, have a list of volunteer interpreters handy for translating the message.)

- **Lunch**
  - Where do students go to eat?
  - Does Bounkham need to bring a lunch or can he buy it at school?
  - Is he aware that the food and way of eating may be unfamiliar?
  - If he buys milk or lunch, is it a cash sale, or is all the money collected on a specific day?
  - What is the procedure in the cafeteria?
  - What do students do when they finish eating?
- **Breaks**
  - Where are students allowed to go during breaks? (In elementary schools, are there special play areas for certain age groups?)
  - Are there any places they may *not* go? (In many high schools one area is designated for seniors only. If Bounkham is not a senior, he needs to know that area is off limits.)
  - How do the students know when it is time to go back to class?
  - What is the procedure for re-entering class?

    In elementary school, do the students line up in a single line, or in separate lines for boys and girls? Do they stand outside the classroom door or in another designated spot on the playground?

    In secondary school, are there one-way halls or is traffic designated to move in one direction on one side and another on the opposite side?
  - When is Bounkham allowed to go to his locker?
- **Getting home**
  - If Bounkham rides the bus, where does he wait for it?
  - How does he tell which bus is his?
  - How does he tell the driver where he needs to be let off?
  - If he is being picked up by family members, where does he wait for them?
  - What should he do if they don't come?
  - Where is a phone if he needs to call his parents or other family members? Is money required to make a phone call?
  - What route does he take to get home if he must walk?
  - Are parents made aware of any child welfare legislation that governs the minimum age at which a child may be at home without adult supervision?

Use Resources Within the School/Within the Community

A teacher with thirty students may not have time to give one new student a comprehensive orientation. Fortunately, even the smallest school can draw on a number of resources that help ease the ESL student's first day. If you are unable to give your students an orientation during the morning break or at lunch (and face it, how many teachers really have an entire break period free?), consider these alternatives.

USE STUDENT HELP

❑ Find another student who speaks the same language. A student who is already familiar with the school and its routines and requirements can explain to Bounkham in his own language what is expected of him, and help him adjust to his new surroundings. Allow that student helper to sit in your class for a day or two to help ease the transition. You can make and use your own orientation checklist using the information that begins on page 11. If Bounkham is in high school, find another student who can be released for the day to help him get from class to class. The first day of school is bewildering enough for incoming freshmen, and must be many times more frightening to one who hasn't experienced North American schools before.

❑ Assign a buddy. Put an English-speaking student in charge of showing him around, making sure he gets from one place to the other and doesn't get lost.

USE ADULT HELP

❑ If your school or district has an ESL teacher, he or she may be able to help guide the student through this first day (or days) at school.

❑ A bilingual teacher or bilingual aide may be able to give the student his first-day orientation to the school.

❑ In the event that you have neither of these available, any sympathetic and patient adult—librarian, parent volunteer, resource teacher, counselor, principal—might be entreated to adjust his or her schedule to make time for your student on that all-important first day.

❑ Consider finding a mentor for Bounkham. Many schools have found adult volunteers who agree to devote weekly or monthly time to students to help them succeed. It can be very beneficial to a new student from another country to have an adult's consistent support as he adjusts.

If Bounkham is one of the first students placed in your school and you have no idea where to find cultural support for him, check these resources in your community:

❑ Cultural support groups already working within the community (for example, Lao Family Community Services, MECHA chapter, International Students' Organizations on college campuses, and so on)

❑ The ESL department at the local college or adult basic education programs

❑ The telephone book—look in the "Easy Reference List of Government and Public Services" or similar listing

❑ Mayors' offices often have an immigrant and refugee component ("Consumer Information," "Constituent Service," "Ombudsman," and so on)

❑ Lawyers, especially ones associated with civil rights groups, pro-bono committees of bar associations, Legal Services Corporation

❑ Voluntary agencies that work in refugee resettlement, such as: international institutes, centers; national religious service groups (i.e., Catholic charities, church world services, world relief refugee services, Mennonite Central Committee); other voluntary agencies, such as the Salvation Army, churches, temples, the public library

❑ For emergency interpreters, AT&T offers a Language Line service in more than 140 languages. This 24-hour service is available in Canada and the United States. If interpreters are in short supply in your school district, this option might be critical. Contact AT&T for more information.

First-Day Teaching

Once Bounkham is placed in an appropriate grade, given a class (or set of classes) and an orientation to the school, you can get down to business. Bounkham has settled into his desk, has taken inventory of his books, pencils and pens, and it's a fairly safe bet that he's not going to bolt for the neighbor's yard. It's social studies time. The other students are getting their books out; he sits, hands folded, quietly watching you. He's ready to learn. But he doesn't speak English, and you don't speak Lao. How will you teach?

If Bounkham speaks no English, you will be able to teach him very little for some weeks. Later you can use different alternatives for individualizing instruction so that your student will be learning at least some basic subjects. But for now, you can help him adjust to the classroom and begin to learn English.

THINGS TO DO TO HELP THE STUDENT ADJUST AND BEGIN TO LEARN

- **Give him a place of his own.** For younger children, this may be a cubicle to keep things in. For older students, it may be a desk or an assigned seat. If the students select their own seats each day, you may have an area where students keep supplies. Show Bounkham where to keep his materials for use in your class. This sense of a personal "space" will make him feel included, which will help prevent him hovering in the doorway until everyone else is seated and ready for class, and allow him to slip to his desk without feeling self-conscious.

- **Give him something definite to do.** This activity does not have to be elaborate, just something to occupy him so that he doesn't have to sit doing nothing while the rest of the class works. Make it a simple task which he can enjoy and achieve some success at.

  Many elementary schools that frequently have ESL children drop in during the school year keep an "emergency kit" of things for a newcomer to do when he first arrives. This kit is filled with magazines, pictures to cut out and color, and items to sort and identify. Many of the manipulables we discuss on page 102 are appropriate for this kit, which may also be used by the student whenever he cannot participate in a particular classroom activity.

  For older students, magazines or books with interesting pictures, such as *National Geographic*, are useful. The students can copy or create labels of item categories, or practice writing their names, family members' names, addresses, and so on. They can also label different items found in a classroom. In content area classrooms, students can label such things as equipment or materials. We advocate supplying students with picture dictionaries, such as the *Oxford Picture Dictionary*, so that they can begin learning new vocabulary immediately. The realistic pictures depict everyday life in and out of school. While this dictionary is acceptable for older children, the number of items on a page might be overwhelming for lower elementary children.

  Don't be dismayed if Bounkham only sits and watches for the first few days or so. It is important that he be able to choose whether or not to become involved. The main thing is to be prepared. Have a kit of worthwhile activities planned and ready—as discussed earlier—so that he doesn't have to sit doing nothing, only to get bored, frustrated, or disruptive. It doesn't take long to put one together, and it will save you a great deal of anxiety and guilt when your new student does show up.

- **Establish a routine.** This makes planning easier because you will follow the same steps each time. For a non-English speaker, everything has to be learned by observing, so routine is essential. Bounkham will feel less self-conscious if he can anticipate what is going to happen in class. And as the process becomes familiar, he will become more inclined to risk error by speaking.

- **Include the student in activities.** The first few days and weeks of school are lonely times when Bounkham may feel alienated and alone. Being part of a group will help him overcome those feelings. Even if he cannot participate fully—or at all—he will benefit from the exposure. A buddy system may decrease the possibility of anxiety and alienation.

- **Seat your ESL students so they have access to you and to their peers.** Strategically, the best place to seat Bounkham is near the front so you can easily monitor his progress with class activities. Don't put him in the first desk in the first row; he will feel center-stage and will also be unable to watch what others do. The second row on the entrance side is probably ideal.

If you have more than one ESL student in your class, grouping them is a good idea as long as they are not isolated; they need access to native-English speakers. The seating arrangement illustrated below gives these students proximity to their peers, and you'll find it easier to monitor your ESL students' progress because they will all be seated in the same location in the classroom.

Grouped seating also enables you to repeat assignment directions, provide more explanation of content, and answer questions. Students are also able to help each other during seat-work time.

Planning for the Year

Setting short- and long-term goals is a good remedy for curing the panic you may feel when a non-English-speaking student is assigned to your class. Mapping out your objectives helps you see that you can achieve realistic goals with this new student; making sure your goals fall into short- and long-term categories keeps you from overwhelming yourself—or him! But don't make any long-term goals for the first few weeks. Bounkham will be adjusting to all the people and things he encounters at the school and may seem to know less English than he actually does. Only when you know you have a good sense of your student and his learning style should you make long-range plans for his curriculum. The following are some steps to help you manage.

PREPARE COPING STRATEGIES

- **Have a game plan.** It is not enough to assume that Bounkham will "pick up" English on his own. He needs you to help him make sense of the new language so that he is able to catch up and work at grade level with his peers.

- **Have expectations.** Expect him to learn. Learning does not stop simply because he is grappling with a new language. Bounkham can learn new words, and he can learn concepts from the activities he participates in. Your expectations of him are positive encouragement that you believe in his potential.

- **Accept the fact that the ESL student will be behind.** If you feel anxiety because you believe Bounkham has to be up with the rest of the class in four weeks, you are setting yourself up for some real misery. Understanding that he will be filtering content through limited language proficiency allows you to focus on the bigger picture and helps you to appreciate his little successes.

ESTABLISH SHORT-TERM GOALS

- **Write down what the new student can and cannot do.** Does Bounkham have good reading skills? Is he able to communicate? Can he write only words or full sentences? Is he able to interact with the other students? How does he handle the assignments you give him? Is he able to demonstrate any prior knowledge in the content area? Will he be required to adjust to a new learning style? For example, will he have to learn to ask a question during class time rather than waiting until class is over? Keep records of his starting points and progress. That way you will know what he needs and you will know how well he is doing.

- **As you are getting acquainted, set some short-term goals for your student based on your observations.** For the first week or so of class, you can focus on getting Bounkham to participate in the classroom routine and begin to use English. This can be anything from acknowledging instructions, to turning in a written assignment. Tailor the goals you set to your perception of his abilities.

- **When teaching the new student to communicate, teach vocabulary that will be useful.** Teach him words and popular idiomatic expressions that he will hear and be able to use immediately. Don't teach vocabulary-list words that have little to do with this student's everyday life. These words are meaningless memory-eaters, and Bounkham could be spending his time more fruitfully on a vocabulary that will give him instant feedback.

- **Teach essential content-vocabulary.** For example, the words *population, community, ecosystem, biosphere, tissue, cells* are fundamental vocabulary to science. This is vocabulary that cannot be simplified. Students need to know these words to read the text and to go on to more specialized or broader knowledge in that particular field. Depending upon Bounkham's level, you can decide how much content-vocabulary he can handle. If his language abilities are very limited, you can focus on classroom vocabulary and basic communication skills.

- **Use audio-visual materials, which are wonderful tools for language learning.** Films, recordings of popular songs, videotapes of educational TV shows, photos, slide shows, and comic strips can all help to develop communication skills.

- **Find out the new student's favorite activities and interests, and develop related assignments that will encourage and develop his attempts at the English language.** English is most effectively learned when generated from attempts to communicate, not from a focus on perfect grammar and syntax.

- **Encourage extracurricular activities as springboards for English acquisition.** Many school clubs and after-school activities can provide firsthand exposure to all kinds of vocabulary in a variety of contexts. If Bounkham wants to play on the school's soccer team, he will be exposed to English vocabulary, used for a game he probably already knows how to play. Whatever club or activity Bounkham joins, the motivation to learn English will arise from his need to contribute to his chosen interest and communicate with others involved.

- **Develop an overall plan.** Now that you know something about your ESL student, develop strategies for the long run. This step might seem self-evident, but it is a critical one. Rather than having "getting through the book" as your objective, envision the course as a whole. What do you want Bounkham to learn?

ESTABLISH LONG-TERM GOALS

- **Establish minimum competencies.** When you know what you want to cover by the end of the semester, decide on a "bottom line" set of concepts your students must learn to pass. You can then evaluate your ESL students using this list. It is easy to assess ESL students in terms of how much they are missing the mark, how much they *don't* know when compared to your regular students. In establishing basic goals, you can measure instead how much they *can* do. For example, for history at the high school level, you may decide the basic concepts to be learned are:

Why people move

What happens when two cultures have to live side by side

How life changed when people moved to a new climate

How people in each era and place made a living

How they governed themselves

Map skills

Time lines

Famous and important people and their contributions

Relate these to Bounkham's own emigration experience. If he is willing, have him share his story with the class.

- **Prioritize your list.** When you have decided what's most important, and Bounkham has not been able to grasp these things, he should not proceed to the next level; if he knows the fundamental concepts, but is missing some of the lesser ones, he should. For example, in a unit on the westward movement, your unit objectives for the class might be that they are able to identify the major components of westward expansion: the reasons for it, its impact on Native Americans as well as other colonial powers, significant dates, and the economic endeavors of the pioneers. If Bounkham understands most of these, he has fulfilled most of your objectives. Even though his map skills may still be weak and he has yet to acquire some of the vocabulary, these skills are of lesser importance and can be learned on the next unit.

- **Select themes for teaching/learning units.** For instance, in history at the junior high or high school level, you can use themes such as expansion, war, waves of immigration, the Colonial era, the Civil War, and so on. (Be sensitive to certain topics/themes that might evoke traumatic and negative emotions.) For science, you might decide to examine a nearby plot of ground throughout the year. Students can gather data at specified times each month, keeping careful records of plant and animal life, the effects of various types of weather, as well as other activity on the land. They can classify species and varieties of life, speculate on changes that might take place, revise their predictions based upon new data gathered. Each successive observation improves their skills, and all benefit from the repetition involved in the study.

  Repetition gives the course a coherent structure and makes each segment successively easier to understand—not only by the ESL students, but by other students as well. Repetition also gives a course shape and symmetry. Often, history or science courses seem little more than a jumble of unrelated facts and dates that are memorized for a test, only to be forgotten immediately afterward.

In an integrated, thematic approach to instruction, students can see the course as a comprehensive whole, related to the world outside and to the people who live in it.

- **Develop a grading structure for literate ESL students.** An evaluation system to mark the progress made by Bounkham reduces gray areas during grading time. As an example, we have included the format one junior high school has adopted for grading within specific marking periods.

This format is ambitious, but if the ESL students are aware that they will be accountable for certain things, they have certain goals to shoot for, rather than a vague "when they learn English."

For more information on grading, refer to chapter 3, page 69.

REQUIREMENTS FOR ESL STUDENTS
CENTRAL JUNIOR HIGH

- **During the first nine weeks, literate ESL students are accountable for**

  All math

  All work done in ESL assignments or with their tutor

  Tasks modified for the ESL student, such as book reports that require the student to take the book a chapter at time and do a simple retelling of the story

  Contributions to group work

- **During the second nine weeks, literate ESL students must**

  Take all work sheets

  Put their names on them

  Do as much as they can

  Hand them in

  (The more advanced students can get a grade after the second nine weeks.)

- **During the third nine weeks, the students must**

  Be able to do almost all the work

  Be graded with others, with some allowances (for instance, if they didn't finish a test because they needed to make constant references to a dictionary, they can finish later in study hall or after school)

Conclusion

The first days with a limited-English speaker in the classroom are the hardest for everyone concerned. At times you may feel that the going is slow, and results are far and few between. Chances are your student feels the same way. Nurture attitudes of patience, compassion, and a sense of humor to encourage the student's process of assimilation. Celebrate the successes no matter how small they may seem. In spite of the frustrations, this can be a rich opportunity for all of you.

TESTING AND PLACEMENT   2

In this chapter, we will provide practical guidelines about

- Where ESL students should be placed
- How to test them

Testing

In the U.S., federal law requires that all students coming from a non-English-speaking background

- Be surveyed within thirty days of enrollment to determine if they speak a language other than English
- Be tested within ninety days of enrollment in their native language, if they are not sufficiently fluent in English

  NOTE: There is no equivalent federal law in Canada. Policies for ESL students are the responsibility of school divisions/ districts or, in some cases, individual schools.

Many school districts do not test, either because they don't know how and are unaware of the test choices they have available to them, or because they have no tests translated into the students' native languages.

There are many tests available, and even in those cases when no standardized tests have been translated into the languages your students speak, it is possible to learn much about your students and their proficiency levels, and make competent decisions about which classes and grade levels to place them in.

INITIAL DECISIONS

Ideally, the school will have been given prior warning that a new ESL student is coming, and whoever is responsible can make unhurried decisions about his placement. Unfortunately, this is often not the case. Parents or guardians will bring the student to the school, medical papers in hand, and leave him there, forcing placement in a classroom without any type of assessment.

The person(s) responsible for the initial testing and placement of ESL students vary remarkably from school to school. Ideally, testing and placement will be the responsiblity of an ESL specialist, or in cases in which no specialist is available, a counselor, special education teacher, or principal. The reality is that these people are often overextended, so the job of testing and placement is handed over to someone else—a teacher, an aide, or a parent volunteer. This is regrettable, as these people are often not provided with the necessary training and sometimes lack the sensitivity for this task.

Before the new student comes to school, or as soon as possible after his arrival, a home language survey should be administered to determine whether he speaks a language other than English at home. In Appendix B, we illustrate a sample survey. An older student can fill this out at school with an adult's help. Younger students are often unreliable about the languages spoken in their homes, so the parents or legal guardians can be asked to fill the survey out. The help of an interpreter/translator is often required.

Placement

To illustrate the issues involved in placement and evaluation, we will track the progress of four students.

Elsie, a nine-year-old from Ethiopia, is brought to school by a church sponsor. Her father was murdered by warring tribes; her mother died of malnutrition in a refugee camp. She is here with her uncle. Due to the political instability in her country, all her records have been lost.

Balint, thirteen, is an immigrant from Hungary. He is a sturdy, friendly boy with a loud voice. His parents are college educated and he has studied English in school.

Li Trang is sixteen, a refugee from Vietnam who has lost all his relatives. He has been adopted by Americans.

Charlie Longclaws is a six-year-old from a reservation in the west. His parents have moved to the city to seek medical help for a younger sister. He is fluent in his native language and has learned some English, but is not proficient.

THE GRADE-LEVEL ISSUE

The school's first job is to place the student in the proper grade with the right teacher.

Elsie, the Ethiopian, is tiny and appears much younger than her nine years. She smiles shyly, but will not speak. The principal is tempted to place her in the first or second grade. Balint, the Hungarian, has had some English, but does not speak it well. The counselor argues that he be placed in the sixth grade because the content is less demanding and he will have an easier time learning the language without the pressure of studying new subjects he has not encountered before. Li Trang's American parents think that he would do well in the tenth grade. Charlie, fresh from a reservation, has not been to school at all. His placement is relatively simple: because of his age he can be put in kindergarten with his peers. His main limitations are his lack of fluency in English and problems associated with adjustment to a new culture and environment.

Their lack of content knowledge and required skills is not reason enough to warrant placement of Balint and Elsie in lower grades. These students should be placed with classmates of their age group for several very important reasons:

❑ Their emotional and social needs can be met only by being with their age-mates. It could be devastating to Balint's ego to place him with younger students, severely affecting both his motivation and self-esteem. Students adapting to a new language and culture are quick to model the behavior of their peers. Sharing common interests with their age-mates encourages and enhances language development. Depriving students of the opportunity to interact with their peers can hinder adjustment to their new life.

❑ Lack of fluency in English does not indicate limited intelligence. Even though these students' lack of English makes them unable to cope with grade-level work at first, they are not necessarily behind in cognitive development. What is more, the English spoken in the eighth grade is not appreciably different than that spoken in the sixth grade. Many students experience boredom and frustration when required to repeat the content they have gained in their first language. It may well be that Elsie, Balint, and Li Trang are perfectly capable of doing work at grade level.

❑ Students beyond the primary grades can often learn to read faster than younger children simply because they are more mature.

❑ More than any other factor, success with ESL students depends upon a commitment by teachers and administrators to acknowledge and meet their special needs. Academic achievement is directly linked to the quality of instruction, not just the placement of the student.

AT THE ELEMENTARY LEVEL

As noted before, Charlie, the six-year-old from the reservation, can be placed in kindergarten with his peers. Most kindergarten curricula blend the development of pre-reading and pre-writing skills with an exploration of the child's world. Activities at this level are predominately hands-on and rich in language-learning opportunities. The teacher will need to allow Charlie more time to demonstrate his mastery of lesson concepts, because he is juggling language learning at the same time as he is adapting to a new culture. For example, Charlie may take longer to correctly identify the colors of a rainbow. First, he will need to learn the English vocabulary for colors, and then to distinguish which colors appear in a rainbow. The teacher must be sensitive to Charlie's unique learning curve and assess his progress appropriately.

With Elsie (from Ethiopia), there is some flexibility. Under certain circumstances, and after careful consideration, it might be permissible to place a child such as Elsie one grade lower than her age-mates (but not more than one). If the school has split or multi-age classes, this would be the best option, as both her affective and cognitive growth would be ensured. Placing Elsie in a class made up of third and fourth grade students would allow her to work with the younger children but socialize with her age-mates in the fourth grade.

What if subsequent testing reveals that Elsie has no skills at all? With no prior schooling, she will be starting at square one. It is very difficult to teach a child who is at the pre-kindergarten level when there are twenty-five other students in the class. The experience would be frustrating, not only for her (because she can't do the work), but for the teacher (who won't have the time to help her). An obvious solution might appear to be placing Elsie in a first-grade classroom where the teacher would be better equipped to handle her needs until she learns her basic skills; however, this choice is not best for the student. For a child like Elsie, being with her age-mates is the most important consideration. She will be able to participate with them in phys. ed., art, music, and during recess and lunchtime, in the process making the friends that are so critical for second-language learning (not to mention, for happiness). But she will need to work with her reading and math peers in those skill areas. This might necessitate going for math and reading to the first-grade classroom or to the school's learning or resource center (if the school has one), or working one-on-one with a tutor, with resource assistance or part-time ESL support. Pulling her out of class or separating her for special help is admittedly not the ideal situation, but offers a balance that responds to her varied needs. Some elementary schools coordinate their "centers," having reading and math at the same time throughout the school. In this way children can move from center to center according to their needs without missing out on other classroom activities.

The placement of Balint (the thirteen-year-old Hungarian immigrant) and Li Trang (the sixteen-year-old from Vietnam) involves other considerations. For the same reasons outlined, both would benefit from placement in the grades appropriate to their ages, with careful selection of the classes they take. There is some leeway in placement depending on: 1) whether there is an ESL teacher; and 2) what tests reveal about Balint's and Li Trang's skills.

If the school has an ESL teacher, Balint and Li could be placed in an ESL classroom or with the ESL teacher for one or two hours a day. If there is no ESL specialist, then other arrangements—aides, peer tutors, and/or volunteers—will have to be made.

If Balint and Li can understand, read, and write English, consider placing them in regular classes all day, with some support from tutors during study periods or after school. Here are some course options:

- Math, a course where ESL students tend to do well, because it is in many ways "language and culture" free

- Science, a "hands-on" course with many opportunities for ESL students to watch and participate with their classmates

- Art, which allows non-English speakers to express themselves in ways other than the verbal

- Music, particularly choir, which relies on a great deal of repetition and provides an emotional outlet

- Phys. ed., which is in many ways language-free (in such games as football or basketball, verbal instructions are "context embedded," that is, the activity is rich in visual cues, and the language the student hears or the instructions given are accompanied by gestures and demonstration)

English is the most important class for instruction in reading and writing. Although we insist elsewhere that reading and writing should take place in *all* classes, this class is the one in which the ESL students will receive most direction in the acquisition of English skills. In language arts, students must be involved in more than simply learning language, they must learn how to use language to learn. According to Chamot and O'Malley (1987), ESL students need to learn study skills that help them succeed in content areas in which course concepts—not the language—are the focus.

For Balint and Li, courses such as history and social sciences should be added later. These courses are "context reduced"—the students cannot rely as much on visual cues to determine the meaning of the content matter. What's more, these subjects require a great deal of reading. When Li Trang and Balint have gained more English proficiency, these courses can be added.

If ESL students' skills are poor, or they come to school illiterate, then remedial help in some form is the only alternative. In situations such as Li Trang's, where his formal schooling has been limited and he may be illiterate, remedial help is probably needed. He will need time to adjust, gain fluency, and complete his required course work. He can take grade nine and/or ten courses without shame, and catch up as his proficiency grows. Some school districts have implemented five-year programs for their ESL students. As some students don't begin to function in class for a year or more, a five-year plan allows them the time they need.

Be sure to consult parents about placement. Many feel strongly that their son or daughter should be placed with their age-mates; others will go along with whatever recommendations you make, as long as they are based on sound assessments, and not solely on the basis of the student's size or a general feeling of "that's where he belongs." Some parents may even want their child placed a grade ahead, believing that the schools in their country of origin are academically ahead of the new school.

Placement is a tricky business. Each placement should be dealt with on an individual basis, taking into consideration the student, his schooling history, his parents' wishes, and what administered tests reveal about his skills.

Assessment Through Testing

Testing is a complex and difficult issue. At the risk of oversimplifying matters, we have established some basic guidelines to help you through the maze of testing procedures and jargon.

Many commercially produced tests are on the market. Some common ones are: the LAS (Language Assessment Scale); the BINL (Basic Inventory of Natural Language); the BSM (Bilingual Syntax Measure); and the IPT (Idea Proficiency Test). Others are also available.

DECIDING WHICH TEST TO USE

Language competency is a very murky area, one that is difficult to measure scientifically. Whether or not standardized tests are valid is a matter of controversy. **Reliable tests should:**

- **Demonstrate who should be labelled** ESL, i.e., who are in need of language services because their English proficiency is low.

- **Be consistent.** If one test shows Balint needs ESL services, it should be possible to corroborate this by other tests.

- **Highlight skills students have mastered**, thereby predicting the students' ability to succeed in regular academic programs.

- **Identify the students' specific linguistic and academic needs.** Do they speak well, but need help in writing? Do they write well, but speak haltingly?

- **Tell you the students' proficiency levels** with the various skills: what grade level they read at, how much they can write, what vocabulary they know, and how much they understand.

- **Have "high content validity"**—do these tests measure what they claim to measure? Often, the validity of tests is confounded by the language proficiency of the test-taker.

WHY TESTS FAIL

You may have heard complaints about commercially produced assessment tests: that they are useless—or worse! We feel it is important for you to understand why these complaints are often based on reality. Frequently, the test results are ambiguous or incorrect; they do not accurately reflect students' English language abilities. These tests fail for one or more of the following reasons:

- **Many of the tests are culturally biased.** One test asks students to identify pictures of an elephant, a dinosaur, a submarine, and a watermelon. Elsie might not know the English word for *bed* or *house* or *table*, but at least she has them in her own language and understands them because of her own life experience. Unless she has seen a watermelon or a submarine (even in pictures), she does not have the equivalent in Amharic. Asking her to identify something she has never seen or experienced is not a fair measure of her English vocabulary.

- **Many tests are linguistically biased**—the instructions are not translated into the appropriate language. For example, when the instructions, "When you hear two words on the tape, tell me if they sound the same or different," are not translated into Amharic or Hungarian, you have no way of telling whether Elsie or Balint actually understood what they were to do—if their answers accurately reflected what they know, or are a response to their inaccurate perception of the instructions.

- **Some tests are too ambiguous;** you cannot determine exactly what they are telling you about your students' competence. For example, if Li Trang leaves blanks on a cloze test, is it because he did not know the appropriate vocabulary word in English, because he did not know the grammatical structure of the word he wanted to use, or because he did not understand the context of the sentence(s) he was to complete?

- **Other tests do not give the speaker from another culture a chance to show what he can do in English, because they include testing on very small discrete points,** giving equal scoring weight to these sections. For instance, one tests the students' ability to distinguish between minimal pairs and phonemes, the discrimination between the smallest units of sound in English, such as *v* and *b* or *sh* and *ch*. This will only tell you which sounds a student does or does not hear. Knowing that Charlie cannot distinguish between *very* and *berry* is of little use to you and of negligible importance in the overall task of learning the language.

- **Many tests have arbitrary cut-off scores, so they don't necessarily measure students' competency.** For example, they might state that a score below 80 percent indicates that the student functions at the "limited proficiency" level. The companies that design these tests use nice, round figures because they are easy to work with. However, there is no direct relationship between the score and the student's actual ability level. Li may score 81 percent on the test, above the test's stated limited proficiency level, but in actuality may function on a limited basis in English. In a similar vein, Balint may achieve a grade of 100 percent on a test, and still not be able to compete with his English-speaking classmates. The test may measure Balint's skill "at a fourth grade level," but it does not measure Balint's ability to cope in the classroom.

- **Many tests provide incomplete information.** Commercial tests should be used only to provide guidelines for placement and to determine if an incoming student will require ESL or bilingual services. These tests are designed to differentiate between those who have enough English to function in the classroom and those who are truly limited in their English. Not all foreign students *are* ESL students, nor are all Native Americans. (Balint might actually know enough English to keep up with his English-speaking classmates.) Use these tests to help with placement, and go elsewhere to find more specific answers to your questions on how well a student reads or writes.

Supplemental Tests

Although in the U. S. you are required to use one standardized test, supplemental tests can be developed to find out other information that teachers really need to know. These supplemental tests should be given by the classroom teacher as this is the person who requires the information.

Individual students' proficiency levels in listening, speaking, reading, and writing vary depending upon their experiences in North America and their own countries. Some might have advanced speaking and listening skills, but poor reading and writing skills. Others might be proficient in reading and writing, but will be able to understand little spoken English, or speak well enough to be understood by others. Therefore, you need to test *all* skills to determine how much your student knows. For example:

Can Charlie speak any English? How much does he understand?

If it is established that Balint has some literacy in English, can he handle the classroom assignments?

Can Elsie read and write?

What specific areas does Li Trang need help with?

Once you have this information, you can decide the course of your instruction and monitor your students' progress. All four language skill areas—listening, speaking, reading, and writing—must be tested.

TESTING HINTS

Before testing, you must have a list of things your students need to know. In the Student Vocabulary Test (Appendix C) we list some survival words and concepts that are important; you can start with these. But vocabulary is just the beginning; you also want to discover whether students can understand and produce extended discourse—speech beyond the word and sentence level. Students' proficiency refers both to their knowledge of the language and their ability to use it.

■ **Try to make test situations as low key and stress-free as possible.** Put your students at ease. Take the time to explain why you are testing them and *why* you are taking notes; some students will be nervous anyway, but this helps to create a less threatening atmosphere.

- Don't take students away from the class for testing when their classmates are involved in "fun" activities.

- When testing, try to ask students to do at least one thing they can succeed at.

- If students can't get through the oral section of the test, don't assume they will be unable to do the written section. Many students who have studied English in school in their countries of origin can read and write much better than they speak (and often put native-English speakers to shame with their knowledge of grammar).

- Stop testing when the students indicate fatigue or frustration. You can always come back to do another segment later.

TESTING LISTENING COMPREHENSION

Test your students' "receptive proficiency"—how much English they understand.

- **Vocabulary.** When testing identification

  □ Use real objects as much as possible. For example, use a desk rather than a picture of a desk.

  □ Use photographs (cut out of magazines or catalogs), not drawings or paintings. Many children, even those from literate North American families, cannot make sense of little whimsical figures or line drawings. Students from non-literate cultures often have great difficulty making a connection between what they see in real life and two-dimensional drawings or paintings.

  □ Using photographs, ask test questions about things that are fairly universal, such as boys, girls, children, trees, clouds, and so on, not about culturally laden objects such as hamburgers.

  □ Ask only one question at a time—don't combine questions. Test for colors, then shapes, but not both at the same time. Have the student look over a page of colored squares, then ask, for instance, "Which is the red square? Which is the blue square?" Don't ask complex questions like, "Where is the red triangle?" then "Where is the black pen?"

- **Simple commands.** Find out if they can understand simple sentences so that they can follow classroom instructions. In items 12 and 17, Appendix C, we list a number of commands they will be expected to know.

Spontaneous speech will elicit a language sample that is most representative of your students' oral language ability. This is best accomplished through an informal interview. Many students are shy and self-conscious, so you can use several methods to encourage them to speak:

- **Ask them questions about themselves** such as, "Do you like to play soccer? Do you like to watch TV? What's your favorite program?" Sometimes information questions can get the ball rolling. "Where are you from? What city did you live in? What language do you speak at home?"

- **Use photographs** from magazines or newspapers. Find a photo of an activity, then ask the student to tell you what the people in the picture are doing. For example, you might use photos of a family eating dinner, children playing soccer, or a farmer working in the fields.

- **Read a story.** Whether you are working with high school students or first graders, this activity is valuable for revealing the students' grasp of the language. Through questioning, you can observe how much oral language the students are able to understand and how well they can reformulate the language they have heard when asked to retell the story. For elementary students, the best type of story to use is one about everyday life. Those learning a new language may find it hard to follow a story line that is not easily predictable from their everyday life experiences. For high school students, short uncomplicated stories or articles work well. You might find some in magazines, in the school paper, or yearbook. If it has been established that the student (Balint, for example) is literate and has studied English, you might consider letting him read the story himself, rather than reading it to him.

After reading the story or article to the students, ask them to tell you about the plot. Be aware, though, that this may leave them stymied, because they don't know where to start. Prompting, in the form of key questions that don't reveal the answer (such as "And then what happened? What was the name of the dog?") is acceptable. One drawback to asking students to retell a story is that if the students are shy, they may simply respond to your questions with "I don't know," for fear of making a mistake. If the students do this, and you know that only shyness and/or their fear of making mistakes is preventing them from answering the questions, abandon the activity and move on to something else.

First, you need to find out if the students can read at all. Once it has established that they are literate, you can determine their level of proficiency.

Although the home language survey should have given you a good indication of the students' level of education, this can be confirmed by giving them something like the written instructions for a writing sample. Place the instructions sideways on the table. If they turn the paper right side up so that the words can be read, they are probably literate. Now ask them to write their name, watching to see how they do it. If they hold their pens awkwardly and write with difficulty, you can suspect they have little experience with reading or writing.

Give the students a brief questionnaire similar to the home language survey (Appendix B) that asks for their names, addresses, dates of birth, and ages, as well as some personal questions, such as those in the oral language assessment. (See Appendix D for an example.) The way in which they answer the questions and fill in the blanks will enable you to make rough assessments of their reading and writing skills.

The following tests each focus on specific areas of language acquisition and should be given by the teacher. While these tests are helpful when trying to determine an appropriate grade level, they by no means provide definitive results. They are most useful for the teacher who must plan short- and long-term learning objectives for the students. Again, observation of the students while taking the tests is invaluable.

- **Cloze tests.** These tests are usually organized according to grade level. They consist of small passages of a text from which approximately every fifth to seventh word has been deleted. Students are asked to read the selection, then fill in each blank with an appropriate word. To simplify scoring, several commercially produced cloze tests allow only one answer for each blank, although in many cases more than one correct or appropriate answer exists. When scoring the test then, disregard the answer list provided and accept any answers that make sense, are appropriate within the context of the story, and are grammatically correct. Ignore incorrect tense and spelling; these are separate issues from comprehension. Most commercially produced cloze tests provide a structured grading format, so be sure to take this into consideration.

  Although a cloze test's main function is to test for reading comprehension, be aware that some students may not be able to fill in blanks for other reasons. The authors gave one cloze test to students and found that some had trouble with one blank due to a misinterpretation of a word. The sentence read, "Each day Mrs.

Brown would pick _____ from her garden to cook for dinner."
The Hispanic students laughed when they got to that line because
the equivalent word to *garden* in Spanish, *jardin*, more precisely
means *flower garden*, and all they could think of was the farmer's
wife picking flowers to cook for dinner. They actually understood
the reading passage well, but lacked the English exposure to fill in
the blank.

If you have an aide who can help translate, we suggest that you
let students fill in blanks using their own language when they
know the answers but can't think of the words in English. You can
then assume that the students can follow the context of the narrative, but are unable to supply the English vocabulary. To illustrate
the variety of answers students may generate, and the insights you
can glean from these mistakes, we have included a sample from
the Boston Cloze Test in Appendix E.

It is also possible to construct cloze tests tailored to specific
needs. This isn't as easy as it sounds, but you may find it worth the
effort. As it takes higher-level reading skills to predict the fill-in
words for a cloze, design the test for a grade level below the one for
which you are testing. For example, if you want to test at the sixth-
grade level, develop text of fifth-grade difficulty. Write a short
paragraph leaving the first sentence (or two) and the last sentence
of the paragraph intact. Then, omit every fifth to seventh word,
leaving a _____ in its place. The more words between the
blanks, the easier the missing words are to predict. Be sure to eliminate more than verbs or nouns. For the test to maintain technical
credibility, the blanks must be random, and there must be sufficient text left for the student to be able to predict the correct words
for the blanks. Ask the students to read the whole story first, then
fill in each blank with a word that makes sense. Follow the scale
below for a grading format.

WORD CHOICE	%	CORRECT LEVEL
Exact	above 50%	*Independent.* Student does not need instruction at the level tested.
	40–50%	*Instructional.* Needs some instruction to acquire basic reading skills.
	below 40%	*Beginning.* Reading skills are minimal or non-existent. Instruction begins at ground level.
Appropriate	above 75%	*Independent*
	60–75%	*Instructional*
	below 60%	*Beginning*

- **Story Retelling.** If you have been trained in miscue analysis, you can use it with your students. If not, you can have students read a story by themselves, then retell the story to you. Their retelling will give you a fairly accurate picture of how much they have understood. As with the oral retelling test, you may have to help the students with prompts. Once again, key questions that lead but don't give the answers away are useful.

We don't recommend having students read the story aloud to you for several reasons:

- ❑ Reading aloud is a separate skill.

- ❑ Being required to read aloud when they are unsure about their reading skills and may be self-conscious about their accents makes the situation uncomfortable, and can often cause students to pay more attention to their pronunciation than their understanding.

- ❑ Students' oral mistakes often don't reflect their comprehension. Many students who make errors may actually be able to understand the majority of the story.

- ❑ As the test-giver, it is easy to get frustrated and be tempted to jump in and help when you listen to students trying to read a passage aloud. It is best to avoid this situation.

The following example contains a story retelling by a high school student whose first exposure to reading was in English. Somaly read *Jacki* by Elizabeth Rice, a story about a cat who raises a baby rabbit with her kittens. The rabbit thinks she is a kitten too until she sees another rabbit, a "stranger," hanging around the barnyard. After seeing her reflection in a water trough, the little rabbit discovers that she is like the stranger, and when she sees him again, knows it is time to leave with him and lead a rabbit's life.

Somaly's retelling:

> *Story about a mother cat was one. He had her baby born—you know—coming out from her. Then about one week or two week they try to open their eye. And then a mother cat had seen rabbit—the little rabbit—and she took her home and living with her family together. You know, and then they live at—in a mother cat home together and rabbit be a cat baby too. And then one cat and one rabbit that stay on the new "starger"—it kind of thing different you know—rabbit and cat stand in the moonlight and they looking something in the moonlight and they saw it. That's it!*

Somaly understood the story line about a cat adopting a little rabbit into its family of kittens. She remembered the details of the kittens opening their eyes and the mother finding the baby rabbit. However, from the point in the story where the "stranger" is introduced, Somaly lost the thread. She was not able to guess the meaning from the context, so she did not understand that the "stranger" was another rabbit. She "fudges" in her retelling: "starger—it kind of thing different you know" and tiptoes around the ending.

Somaly demonstrated she had understood many parts of the story. She also showed some language skills when she retold that part of the plot involving the rabbit's relationship with the cats. Somaly's retelling would allow the assessor to see that she had some basic reading skills, but that she would need much more reading practice and vocabulary exposure to develop those skills. This information would help her teacher find a starting point for class work.

Story retelling requires that students use English to repeat the story they've heard or read. As their poor speaking skills may not allow them to communicate what they actually understood, the tester must keep in mind that story retelling is not a precise measuring instrument, but only a tool that will provide some insight into students' reading abilities.

- **Writing samples.** Writing samples help determine students' ability to communicate coherently in writing.

    Obtaining and assessing a spontaneous writing sample, which reflects the student's genuine response to a subject he has an interest in or experience with, is the best way to assess the writing ability of students.

    Give students several topics to choose from and a set amount of writing time (fifteen minutes for younger students; thirty minutes for older students). Topics might include writing about: *Something you like to do, Your family, Your first day in this school,* or *Something frightening that happened to you.* (See chapter 6, "Writing," for a more detailed discussion of writing assignments.)

    Your scoring criteria for this sample should be prioritized, beginning with the most important writing skills—which involve communicating the message—and ending with mechanics. It is easy to be dismayed by a paper filled with grammatical or spelling errors, but

TESTING WRITING PROFICIENCY

Michael's Writing Sample

My Family
I have a lot of people in my family. I have a sister and two brothers. and of corse a MoM and DaD. Their names are Andy and Lindee Jeremy, Nathan — Brianna and I Michael My Family and I like to go on trips. We went to a lot of places, We've went to Yosemite, Disneyland, Donner Lake, Texas, and much, much more. I Love my family and my baby sister Brianna a hole, hole lot.

My family.

My family ane big and little They learn.
Some booK I have three sisters and six. brothers. I have my little brothers. Was two years old.

Wang's Writing Sample

these surface errors should not outweigh more critical factors.

Compare the ESL student's writing on this page (Wang's) with the writing of an English-speaking student of the same age (Michael) on the previous page. Although a first glance at an ESL student's writing sample may lead the assessor to believe the student is able to communicate very little, a more careful review using a set of skill priorities may demonstrate that the student actually knows quite a bit. See below and facing page for a detailed comparison between Michael's and Wang's writing.

In Appendix F we give a detailed form to use when rating writing samples. A student whose writing sample receives the "beginner" rating in any of the five categories is significantly limited in his ability to write English.

THIRD-GRADE WRITING COMPARISON

MICHAEL (native-English speaker)	WANG (ESL student)
Content Topic is developed Specific details are provided Adequate description given	**Content** Topic is developed Specific details are provided Adequate description is given
Organization Opening sentence is included Very orderly, moved from one example to the next Transitions used Closing is included sentence	**Organization** Opening sentence is included Evidence of organization All sentences are relevant to topic Concluding sentence has been omitted
Vocabulary Effective word choices made and correct use of word forms	**Vocabulary** Limited, but correct, use of words. Word choice is clear
Language Skills One grammar error is made, but there is overall control of agreement, etc. Good sentence variety used Effective use of word forms	**Language Skills** Some agreement problems Very simple construction Word order is correct Knows sentence boundaries
Mechanics Some spelling errors made Has control of most punctu- ation (commas, periods)	**Mechanics** One spelling error made Periods are not in the correct places

Michael's writing sample was a first draft. He develops the topic of his family by listing the people in his family, describing the things they do together, and concluding with a statement telling us how he feels about his family. Michael moves easily from one point to another, uses age-appropriate word choice and complex sentence structure. Michael makes an error in verb tense, (*we've went*), but it is unclear from his writing sample whether this was due to lack of proofreading or because he didn't know the correct participle to use. He makes a few spelling errors, (*corse* and *hole*), but they are phonetically logical and typical of a first draft effort.

Wang also began his writing sample with a description of his family. He describes what his family does, how many people are in his family, and, like Michael, he ends with the youngest. The topic development and organization is simple, but clear. Wang plays it safe with his word choice and uses very simple sentence construction, but he is able to communicate. The word in the first sentence which, at first glance, looks like *one*, is really *are*, and when Wang read his sample to Barb, he read it as *are*, saying he made the loop too long. Allowing for that error, *My family are big and little* makes sense and communicates. Wang's word order choices are good. For the most part, tense and subject-verb agreement are correct. An additional first reaction to Wang's sample would be to say that he did not know where to begin and end sentences. We would disagree. From Wang's sample, it is evident that he was well aware of the concept of sentence boundaries, (that sentences contain complete thoughts). However, he has not mastered the idea of placing periods to denote those boundaries. Therefore, we assessed this as an error in mechanics and not one in language skills. We learned much about Wang's ability from his writing sample:

He can develop an idea or topic.

He can communicate clearly using simple constructions.

He can state a complete thought.

He needs much practice in writing. LEA (Language Experience) would be a helpful tool.

Wang's control of English allows him to communicate his thoughts. His abilities are similar to Michael's in the areas of content, organization, and vocabulary. Mistakes in the areas of language skills and mechanics are where non-native speakers differ most from native speakers. New language learners have to juggle new forms and constructions, word order, tense, and so on. They may know what they want to say, but get bogged down with English language conventions in their attempts to express themselves coherently.

Making Use of Test Scores

The standardized assessment tests, in addition to the school's own supplemental tests, can provide information about what your students are capable of understanding and producing. However, it is unrealistic to think that scores from these tests will tell you everything you need to know about the new students. Their main purpose is to give the teacher a sense of how to begin to plan for the newcomers in the classroom.

As we have stated earlier, the labels students are given are frequently inaccurate and do not take into account that each student is an individual. If you feel overwhelmed by all the data the test scores generate, and for teaching purposes you need a place to start your planning, you can begin with the following broad categories. They allow you to prescribe goals and objectives for your students based upon their English competency.

CATEGORIZING STUDENTS

- **NES (Non-English speaking).** These students may know how to say their names but very little else. They can answer some questions, but only with one-word answers. In writing, they are able to write their names or make a few scrawls.

  Strategy: These students need one-on-one tutoring, buddies, concrete vocabulary. Include them in classroom activities such as art, sports, and games.

- **LES (Limited English speaking).** These students understand between 25 and 30 percent of what they hear. They can repeat some phrases and know a few catch phrases, but cannot communicate enough to meet their own needs. When writing they make many errors in grammar, spelling, and usage.

  Strategy: Assimilate these students into the school routine. Modify lesson plans.

- **Intermediate.** These students can understand between 50 and 60 percent of what they hear. They can answer questions and generate some language, but only with many inaccuracies. They have mastered the survival words and important phrases. In writing, they make many errors.

  Strategy: Begin to make these students accountable for class work but continue special support for "gaps" and weak areas.

- **Advanced.** These students can understand most of what they hear, and can read and write effectively. They can understand directions given in the classroom.

  Strategy: Make these students accountable for class work, but continue special support for "gaps" and weak areas.

Follow-up

Be prepared to informally re-evaluate ESL students as they become familiar with the school and class routine. Because students are often apprehensive about tests, or feel inhibited in a new environment, their English ability may seem weaker than it is. They often show their true colors only after they relax and feel more secure. You may find you have to adjust your materials up a level or two as your students adjust to the daily routine. In Appendix G, we have included sample IEP (Individualized Educational Plan) forms for the four students we've used as examples in this unit, to demonstrate how courses of instruction might be implemented.

Conclusion

Testing and placement are issues with lots of "gray" areas—no clear-cut foolproof answers. Remember that evaluation of test results must be based on the particular student being assessed. Be prepared to be flexible. We have attempted to provide some guidelines, but most decisions must be made on a case-by-case basis, depending on what you and your administrators, the students and their parents feel are best.

LANGUAGE LEARNING — STUDENTS AND TEACHERS

3

In this chapter, we will discuss principles of second language learning. We will focus on

- Priorities for teaching

- The factors that influence how fast and how well a newcomer learns English

- Behavior and what affects it

- Facilitating cultural adjustment in the classroom

- Teacher strategies that help to maximize learning

- Grading of ESL students

A Comparison of Two Language Programs

We wanted this chapter to be more than a simple presentation of facts and theories, so we decided to illustrate the principles of second language learning in the form of an anecdotal history of Barb's experience as an elementary and secondary level ESL teacher. Although much of the discussion centers on her experiences at the lower levels, the principles can be applied to the secondary level as well.

For three years Barb taught ESL in a small midwestern town adjacent to a large university. The foreign population in the university's married housing complexes was so large that each "village" had its own elementary school with its own resident ESL teacher. Barb was responsible for ESL in all the other schools in the district—five elementary and two middle schools.

With twenty-five to thirty students in eight grades in seven different schools, Barb had only limited time available to spend with each student—pulling the younger children out of their regular classes for perhaps an hour and a half each week, the middle-schoolers for an hour each day. With such limited access to an ESL specialist, each student was integrated within the classroom, working alongside his classmates. When the newcomer could not keep up with his English-speaking peers, Barb would supply the teacher with supplemental activities to keep him busy. All students were mainstreamed and took part in regular classroom activities as best they could.

Although the pull-out program had its drawbacks—particularly as the students had limited time with a trained ESL teacher and were mainstreamed immediately without any survival English—the students, by and large, did very well. The teachers worked hard to provide them with the best opportunities for learning English.

During her third year, Barb was transferred to a position as full-time ESL teacher at one of the university housing-village schools. This school, instead of using the same kind of pull-out program found in the other district schools, had implemented a self-contained classroom where all ESL children needing assistance spent half the day, returning to their classrooms in the afternoon for math, phys. ed., music, and art.

On the surface, this program looked ideal. There were several positive features.

❑   All ESL children were given half a day in the self-contained classroom to work specifically on their English.

❑   Class size was considerably reduced for regular teachers by having the ESL children spend the morning with another teacher. Thus, classroom teachers could concentrate on their English-speaking students without being held back by children who did not have the understanding to keep up with the mandated curriculum. They were not burdened by the extra preparation and explanation time required when working with ESL children.

❑   The ESL students were able to work with a teacher who was specially trained in teaching ESL. This appeared to be much preferable to remaining in a class for most of the day with a teacher untrained in ESL methodology.

❑   The ESL classroom provided a safe haven for the children—a place just for them, where they could feel secure, wanted, and cherished, with a teacher who could give attention to their needs, rather than being lost in the crowd competing against children who could speak the language of instruction.

This school's program is similar to many others, and many schools searching for ways to meet the needs of ESL students find it an appealing option. A teacher with a third or more of her students unable to speak English is faced with a double load: trying to meet the needs of both groups, but at the same time being required to finish the mandated curriculum by June.

Although there were many positive features to this program, there were also many negative effects due to the reality of the classroom situation.

❑   Barb was responsible for more than twenty-six children, from grades one through five, from nine different language groups: Spanish, French, Portuguese, Chinese, Japanese, Korean, Hindi, Farsi, and Indonesian. Some, like first-grader Guillermo, had been in the country for over a year, having come to school as a kindergarten student. Others, like fifth-grader Chatphet, arrived in the middle of November, having spent five years in an Indonesian school. Six-year-old Vaji was slow to catch on to the concept of reading though she spoke well. Ten-year-old Helga, a smart aggressive learner, was ready to take on content material in the new language. Third-grader Yoichiro could read well in Japanese, but resented being in America and fought against learning any English. Quiet, gentle second-grader Laban, who could read Chinese, rarely spoke, but made the transition from Chinese to English with stunning ease.

This range in age, in needs, and in students' ability to speak and read in English, made planning extremely difficult. Twenty-six students meant twenty-six different challenges. Grouping was the obvious answer. But how? According to age? Competence in speaking? Grade level in reading? And what would Barb teach them? How to say hello? What an umbrella was? Colors? Helga and Chatphet were going on to the middle school the following year. Spending time making cut-outs of umbrellas on a rainy day was a waste of their valuable time. They needed to do more than learn only grammar or vocabulary. Barb needed to fill in the academics that were being missed while they were away from their classroom, because a year spent learning only English was a year lost to subject matter.

❑   Barb had two bilingual aides, Spanish-speaking Emma and Midori from Japan. Both were intelligent, dedicated women who worked hard to make the atmosphere pleasant and the learning experience a successful one for each child. Neither, however, was a native-English speaker, and neither spoke perfect English. This meant that for the majority of the day, the children listened to

English spoken either by their classmates who had not fully learned English, or by adults, two of whom had not fully mastered English either. The models the children were exposed to were not adequate or appropriate for their needs.

❑ The friendships that formed in the ESL class, extended to the playground and after school. For example, Japanese boys played only with each other, talking in Japanese. Several of the little girls in the class made friends, but only communicated in rudimentary English sentences, which were rarely extended and enriched by exposure to the English of their peers.

❑ The solution to meeting the needs of all students was grouping, which was a compromise between age, reading ability, and language competence. However, since each child was working at a different level, all needed constant supervision. The student–teacher ratio was about eight to one, larger than the optimum ratio for a situation such as this when each student was working on a different level.

❑ Most important, these children were isolated, segregated from their peers, away from the mainstream for that portion of the day when most of the content and skill development took place, listening only to their teachers and the imperfect English of other newcomers. Lack of access to fluent English models significantly slowed both their English acquisition and their assimilation. The process of acquiring enough "coping" English took much longer.

What We Know About Language Learning

Even though the self-contained program was set up with the best of intentions, the teachers who originated and supported it were operating under certain assumptions that run counter to what we know about language acquisition. We have outlined some of these ESL learning myths:

INCORRECT ASSUMPTIONS

❑ Language must be taught.

❑ Input in the new language must be sequenced and carefully controlled.

❑ The language teacher is in the best position to decide what vocabulary and concepts to introduce, and when to do so.

❑ Newcomers need to master English before they can learn any subject matter.

❑ Once students have learned the language of instruction—in this case, English—their problems in the classroom are largely over and they should be able to handle their academic assignments with no difficulty.

❑ Regular classroom teachers are not equipped to give their ESL students the best opportunities for language learning.

In the past twenty years or so, a great deal of research has been done on first-language and second-language acquisition. This research has revealed that

■ **The second language is learned best when the setting is natural.** Communication is a two-way street; there is a speaker who has something to say and a listener who wants to hear it. Without these three components—speaker, listener, and message—there *is* no communication. Learning a language is much more than just learning the vocabulary or the grammatical rules, it's knowing how and when to use those rules—even in ordinary conversation. This may seem self-evident, but much of the second-language teaching that has gone on in schools ignores this fact and simply teaches vocabulary and rules, resulting in students who can conjugate verbs but cannot carry on a simple conversation.

■ **Students learn from their peers.** Because the use of language is first and foremost a social activity, students learn best from those they work, live, and play with every day. They learn to make sentences and interact in order to meet their social needs: to make friends, to be included in games, to express themselves. No matter how dedicated and resourceful the teacher is, he or she cannot provide the kind of input that learners need so that they can learn how to use the language in real-life situations. The language that students learn from their peers is a *living* language; they have learned it only by and through communicating within situations that are important to them.

■ **Although second-language learners usually learn certain forms in a set order** (such as the -*ing* ending on verbs before they learn the articles *a, an, the*), **presenting language in a sequence** (such as the present tense first, then the past tense) **is *not* the most effective way of teaching.** This method ignores the needs of the learner by limiting his exposure to as much grammar and vocabulary as can be easily presented and practiced at one time. Students may need to say things such as, "I took my mother to the doctor yesterday, so I couldn't come to school," or, "I am going back to Mexico for a few weeks. I'll be back after Christmas." They may need to comprehend advanced language forms such as "If you don't hand in all your assignments, you'll get an F." Sequencing forms rigidly, teaching structures one at a time, and proceeding only when the structure is learned (the way many of us were taught foreign languages) limits students' ability to function within all the situations they might encounter.

■ **A new language is learned best when the primary focus is on the meaning, not the form.** In other words, students learn how to make friends, satisfy their own needs, and learn new things by *using* the language, not by perfecting grammatical forms (such as tenses) one at a time. Learners make mistakes; this is a natural part of learning anything. However, with practice, they gradually get better at figuring out the rules. Communication comes first, then grammatical rules are learned as a part of learning to communicate effectively, not the other way around.

■ **Non-native-English speakers do not need to master English by studying it formally as an isolated activity before they can begin regular class work.** Language can be learned through content material as long as the material is understandable.

■ **There is a misperception that speaking English well will equip ESL students to handle regular class work.** Research has shown this is not necessarily so. It often takes five to seven years to achieve sufficient fluency in academic English to compete on a par with other English-speaking students. To hold students in ESL classes or special programs until they are fully proficient in all areas is unrealistic, impractical, and, in the end, impossible.

■ **Although support from bilingual or ESL personnel is helpful and important, it is not enough.** The classroom teacher, provided he or she employs appropriate methods for teaching non-English speakers, and supplies both understandable situations and opportunities for the student to interact with classmates, is a key factor in the success of the ESL student.

ACCELERATORS AND ROADBLOCKS TO LANGUAGE LEARNING

Accelerators

It's easier when...

- The purpose of using language—reading, writing, speaking, and listening—is real and natural

- The focus is on communication

- There are lots of opportunities to talk and interact with native-English speakers

- Talk is about interesting topics

- Mistakes are a part of learning

- Language is always used—or studied—within a context, not as isolated letters, words, or sentences

- Language has a purpose for the learner

- Students speak only when they're ready

- Sufficient time is provided

Roadblocks

It's harder when...

- The reasons given or situations created for using language are artificial

- The focus is on the form, not on the function (communication)

- ESL students are isolated

- Talk is dull and uninteresting

- Mistakes are bad, and it's more important to get it right than to get a message communicated

- Language is studied out of context

- The particular use of language studied or assigned is irrelevant for the learner

- Students are forced to speak

- Students are pressured to complete work or make progress

A Quality Program

The two programs discussed—the pull-out program versus the self-contained ESL classroom—were widely divergent solutions to the challenge of teaching ESL students. Each had positive features, but neither was ideal. The pull-out program provided small-group tutoring on gaps in learning, and individual help with class work. The self-contained program attempted to deal with the linguistic needs of the students in an intensive way.

If neither the pull-out program nor the self-contained classroom were satisfactory, what constitutes a quality program? How are students' needs best met? Certainly students—and teachers—need support from trained specialists.

"A quality program for second-language learners will neither segregate all students until they are 'fit' to join their peers, nor will it place them in a regular classroom with the expectation that they will learn all they need to learn on their own...." writes Jean Handscombe, (1989). "The ideal is a program that supports second-language students' learning for the entire day."

What often happens in both pull-out and self-contained classrooms is that the ESL teacher assumes the entire responsibility (and the blame) for the ESL students, and the time spent with this specialist is regarded as the "real" learning time. During the remainder of the day the students simply mark time until they are proficient enough to participate fully in classroom activities.

THE COOPERATIVE ROLES OF LANGUAGE AND CONTENT TEACHERS

In the face of the growing populations of non-English-speaking students, the traditional roles of the classroom teacher teaching content and the language teacher teaching language have become rigid, artificial, and inefficient.

What is needed is

- **A common agenda.** Language is everybody's business and everybody's responsibility. This means regular classroom teachers should adapt their curriculum and their teaching style to include students who are less than proficient in their English.

- **A partnership between the ESL and the classroom teacher.** The ESL teachers can offer their expertise on language learning and second language methodologies, while classroom teachers can offer their knowledge of the content to be covered and skills to be learned.

At the elementary level, this means children are integrated within the classroom with their English-speaking peers, and the ESL teacher works in that classroom on concepts that the rest of the class is learning. In some schools the ESL teacher team-teaches with content teachers. Regular meeting and planning times are priorities to ensure that both the students' language needs and content needs are being met, and that both teachers are making maximum use of their time and energy.

At the high school level, support through one or more ESL classes per day is probably necessary at first, but once again the coordination of objectives is paramount; the ESL teacher can reinforce concepts taught in the content classes.

For instance, as we discuss in chapter 8, "Content Area Instruction," content teachers should define and identify the minimum amount of knowledge and competency to receive a passing grade for the class—knowledge of the essential words and concepts. Armed with this knowledge, the ESL teacher can review these with the students, accurately diagnosing content and language deficiencies. Language structures can be taught within the framework of these lessons, making them both usable and useful: for history classes, they can work on correct use of the past tense; for science classes, they can work on cause and effect, and *what if* questions.

One method that is gaining credence among ESL professionals is the "Sheltered English" approach. This is an instructional process used to teach subject matter in an understandable way to students whose English is not sufficiently proficient to manage in regular content courses. It is not "watered down" content, it is content offered at the language level of the student. History, for instance, is taught in high school using a lower grade-level book to a class of only ESL students. The students study the same content as regular history classes do, and receive credit for completing a requirement for their high school diploma. While Sheltered English is strictly for ESL students, you can use many of the strategies in your regular content area classes without sacrificing the needs of your regular students. We demonstrate how in chapter 8.

Learners and Teachers

Language learning is a balance between the learner and the language-learning environment, between "input" and "intake." *Input* is the language the student hears and encounters daily. *Intake* is how much of this input he actually processes and acquires. On the input side of the equation, there is the teacher, the amount and quality of his or her training, the materials and methods used, and the manner in which (and how often) the teacher corrects errors. The climate within the classroom is important: Do the learners feel accepted and free to try out their new language without fear of ridicule and punishment? Another factor is the amount of exposure the student gets to the language: Does he hear it only at school, going home to speak his native language? Does he get input only from the teacher? Or does he have English-speaking friends who will talk to him and guide him through the linguistic maze?

A teacher can provide an optimum environment and still have his or her students learn at different rates and with varying degrees of success. This is because so much learning is dependent on the students themselves. Regrettably, input does not necessarily equal intake.

Intake—The Learner

On the intake side, there are many factors that influence how much language the learner is able or willing to learn: factors within the learner, and factors related to the learner's culture. First we will discuss several of the most important variables within the learner. Researchers Marina Burt and Heidi Dulay (1982) term the psychological factors that allow in or screen out the incoming language, the "affective filter."

- **The learner's personality.** Is this student outgoing and confident, or withdrawn and shy? Carmen is very talkative and attempts to make herself understood by using gestures and examples. She is very motivated and interested in opportunities to express herself. She participates in any activity gladly, studies hard, and jumps into conversations, laughing when she stumbles or makes mistakes. Hoa, on the other hand, is shy and quiet. He doesn't seem to be very active outdoors, except that he enjoys the solitary activity of riding his bike. He needs to be coaxed to talk and to become involved in activities. By the end of her first year in her new school, Carmen is able to take part in all classroom work, while Hoa is just beginning to make headway.

- **Motivation.** Does the learner really want to know this new language? Ana tells her tutor time and again that she doesn't *want* to learn English. She anticipates going home to Mexico very soon. Her progress is very slow and she forgets what she learned the day before. Qais, however, wants to learn English in a hurry. As the older son, he must help his family adjust to life in America, interpreting at the doctor's office or with the landlord, buying groceries, and paying bills. He also wants to make friends and get into the swing of things as quickly as possible, and one way to speed this process up will be to learn English.

- **Age.** Mary knows of one family of seven that came from Laos. The children's ages ranged from eight to thirty. They had all been in the United States for the same amount of time and had all attended English classes. The younger ones were able to speak well enough within the year to translate for the older ones. By the second year, they had little accent and were making great strides in catching up with their peers in class. The older children did not progress nearly as well.

  Teachers intuitively sense—and they see this in their classes constantly—that younger learners learn better and faster. But some researchers claim that older learners are more successful over the long haul. Others, such as Stephen Krashen (1983), believe that what is operating is the difference between "acquisition versus learning." Younger children simply learn differently than older ones. Little ones acquire their second language much like they do their first: by listening, understanding, and eventually speaking—largely an unconscious process. They aren't aware that they are learning the language; they are simply aware that they are communicating. While older learners do a great deal of "acquiring" too, they also seem to need to learn language consciously, sometimes painstakingly, by learning vocabulary and the grammatical rules.

The age factor in language learning is a murky area that has not been satisfactorily clarified by experts. Partly because they are motivated to make friends and have few inhibitions about making mistakes, young children jump right into learning the new language. Older learners, however, have many other things on their minds. They have responsibilities to school and family, and cannot devote the same amount of time to focus on learning. Older learners are also less willing to experiment with new forms, and more interested in "saving face," playing it safe with linguistic structures they are sure of, rather than embarrassing themselves in front of native-English speakers. Older learners also have more linguistic demands placed on them than younger ones. Young children are usually only required to communicate orally, and their language skills can grow along with their minds as they grapple with more and more sophisticated ideas. Adolescents and adults are required to use more complex types of language to coincide with the complex reasoning processes demanded by school and society. These language skills take much longer to acquire than the usual interpersonal language skills that are needed to get by on the playground or in the street.

- **State of mind.** How your student is feeling, how stable his life is, how preoccupied he is with such emotions as loneliness, homesickness, and culture shock or with outside distractions such as family responsibilities, profoundly influence his ability to absorb and utilize the input he is receiving.

This last variable is extremely complex. Often the things that affect your student's state of mind are either beyond his control or operate at an unconscious level. These factors are so important that we have devoted the entire next section to them.

FIRST ENCOUNTERS WITH MAINSTREAM NORTH AMERICAN LIFE

Moving is difficult under any circumstances. For some of us, moving across town, away from familiar scenes and faces, can be a wrenching experience. How much more those feelings are magnified for students who come from halfway around the world! The changes ESL students have to cope with are many and great, and these can have a far-reaching effect on their assimilation.

- **A change in geography and climate.** Students from tropical southeast Asia, for example, relocated to places such as Minnesota, are unprepared for the severity of the winters.

- **A change from rural to urban settings.** Refugees from the farms of Cambodia and Laos have found themselves thrust into inner-city tenements with few trees or birds, without even a tiny plot of land to till. Native Americans from reservations find themselves having to adjust to the big city.

- **A change in the size of the living environment and/or the economic situation.** Many refugees, often farmers or previously well-to-do businessmen, have lost everything and arrive in this country with only the clothes on their backs. Families are crowded into tiny apartments, and students and their parents work long hours at minimum wage or less just to survive.

- **A change in social status or opportunities and goals.** A number of refugees, such as many of the Cubans and Vietnamese, were the elite, well-educated professionals in their home countries. Now they find their licenses or degrees are not valid in North America. Doctors, dentists, veterinarians often can find work only as gardeners or factory workers, unable to make the most of their skills.

- **The reason for the changes.** Although many new immigrants come to the United States or Canada to find a better life, others fled their countries out of fear for their lives, not out of a desire to live elsewhere. For them, the move was a forced choice. In the words of one expert, "An immigrant leaves his homeland because the grass is greener; a refugee leaves because the grass is burning under his feet." Thus, refugee students often have emotional ties to their homeland, and continue to nurture the hope of returning there, only allowing themselves to become marginally involved with their new home.

- **The change itself.** For many, the move has been traumatic, if not life-threatening. One can only guess at the experiences some students, even very young ones, have been through. Some have seen their parents murdered or their families separated by war. Some must deal with the guilt of being the child chosen to live, while their siblings were left behind to face certain death. Many have lived through days at sea on unseaworthy boats without food or shelter; others have walked hundreds of miles to safety. Many have left loved ones behind and are faced with the anxiety of not knowing whether these people are still alive. They live in a sort of limbo, waiting for their lives to right themselves somehow.

- **A change in the language.** This last element compounds the loss of a student's lifestyle and homeland. Being unable to speak English slows students' ability to adjust to North America. They can't understand the school routine. They can't make friends easily. They can't fit in. They have no one to "show them the ropes" and, most important, no one who is able to provide the emotional support and reassurance that they are accepted.

CULTURE AND CULTURE SHOCK

While students are individuals, they are also members of the particular culture they were born into. The culture of a society embodies elements that are tangible: the clothing, food, festivals, social customs, and so on. It also encompasses the intangible elements: the values of the society, its world view, its attitudes concerning life and death. Our culture helps define us mentally and spiritually. It also dictates how we interact with society.

Many students from other cultures—including our own Native Americans—are confronted with the awesome task of functioning in a society they don't understand. There is a mismatch between our culture and theirs. Their own culture has a different set of norms for simple things we take for granted, things such as how to address the teacher, how close to stand to the person they are talking to, how loud to talk. Many times what they see and hear in North America is in direct conflict with their own set of cultural values: people sitting with their legs crossed so that the soles of their feet are showing, dating, displaying affection in public, openly questioning a teacher's point of view. They often feel confusion, conflict, and helplessness over the wide disparity between what they have hitherto unquestioningly believed was right and what they experience in everyday North American life. These feelings are defined as "culture shock."

Faced with the task of coming to terms with this new culture, students must decide for themselves how they want to fit in, and what kinds of compromises they are willing to make in order to succeed.

Becoming acculturated to the mainstream North American way of life can mean conflict. Many feel that they must abandon the old ways. Children, more adaptable than their parents, embrace our culture more readily, which can lead to tension between the generations. Hibe from Saudi Arabia, for instance, began school at five. She was outspoken and sociable, expressing her opinions in a forthright manner. This was the cause of real worry for her parents who were committed to Muslim ways, including the submissive place of women in their society. What North American schools encourage and what her parents believed was acceptable were in direct conflict. Gaida, who came at age eleven, threw herself into the North American lifestyle, becoming a cheerleader and a star on the girl's volleyball team in high school. By the time her parents returned to their country when she was nineteen, she could no longer fit into the traditional society she had been born into, and chose, against her parent's wishes, to stay in America.

DIFFERENT CULTURAL BEHAVIORS

Sometimes our customs conflict with theirs and we are not always quick to notice the mismatch, because these are automatic behaviors—things we do without thinking.

Following is a list of some of the cultural behaviors that differ significantly from ours:

- **Avoiding eye contact.** This is considered polite and respectful behavior in some cultures, such as Laotian, Hmong, or Hispanic. However, a teacher might consider a student who looks down at the floor uncooperative or sullen. How many times do we say to children we are scolding, "Look at me when I'm talking to you!"

  Avoiding eye contact can have serious consequences for older students and adults. Mary had several high schoolers who were turned down for jobs they were qualified for because the employer thought they weren't listening or paying attention to what he said, although they were merely showing respect by keeping their eyes downcast.

- **Different attitudes about cooperation.** Some students come from cultures that are based on the premise that people help each other. They are unaware that in our schools helping a fellow student with a problem may be construed as cheating. Many Polynesian, Native North American, and Southeast Asian cultures are this way.

- **Fear of making mistakes.** For some students, making a mistake is a greater error than leaving a question unanswered or asking another student for help. For some students, such as the Japanese, ultimate correctness is always the primary objective.

- **Fear of being singled out for individual praise.** In many cultures, such as Southeast Asian and Native American, the group or the family is always seen as more important than the individual.

- **Different role expectations for boys and girls.** This attitude is most prominent among students who come from countries that have ascribed different roles to women and men, such as the Muslim countries of the Middle East. Problems arise if the students are unused to having a teacher of the opposite sex; they may react with some awkwardness towards the teacher or they may be openly disrespectful.

- **High or low motivation to achieve academically, based on gender.** This is related to the item above. In some cultures only males are expected to do well; the females simply mark time. They are in school as a formality, not to achieve any real learning goals.

- **Uneasiness with the informality of classroom atmosphere.** Public behavior in certain cultures is always formal. Many European schools, such as those in Germany, or Asian schools, such as those in Japan, are very strict, to us, almost militaristic. They often view North American schools as bordering on chaos, and the informality an invitation to misbehave. Teachers who wear jeans, sit on their desks, and put their feet up are viewed as extremely impolite.

- **Uneasiness with our North American school system.** Related to the issue above, newcomers are often uneasy about the child-centered, process-oriented curriculum and educational practices of our school systems, as opposed to the more traditional subject-centered learning environments found in most countries of the Old World and the Far East.

- **Taboos toward certain physical contact.** For Buddhists, the area around the head and shoulders is sacred, and it is considered impolite for another person to touch these areas. Therefore, a reassuring pat on the shoulder from the teacher may be interpreted as an affront by the student.

- **Beliefs about the propriety of certain kinds of dress.** Certain cultures have rigid customs as to what is proper and improper dress, particularly for girls. As a result, for instance, the clothes students must wear for gym and the requirement to take showers may cause a great deal of distress for students.

Anyone who moves to a different area, whether it is within their immediate neighborhood, town, state or province, or country, experiences to some degree the same four stages as they become adjusted to their new surroundings. There are many names for

THE STAGES OF ACCULTURATION

these stages, but the easiest to remember are the four H's: honeymoon, hostility, humor, and home.

- **Honeymoon.** This stage takes place when people first arrive. It is characterized by extreme happiness, sometimes even by euphoria. This is especially prevalent with refugees who have finally arrived safely in North America. For them, their new home is truly the land of milk and honey.

- **Hostility.** After about four to six months, reality sets in. These people know a bit about getting around and have begun learning the ropes, but this new place is not like their home: they can't get the food they are accustomed to; things don't look the same; they miss the life of their home country, the familiar places and faces and ways of doing things. Gradually they begin to feel that they hate North America and want to go back to their home country, no matter how bad things were there. This stage is often characterized by complaining; wanting to be only with others who speak their language; rejecting anything associated with the new culture, such as the food, the people, even the new language; feeling depressed and irritable or even angry; having headaches or feeling tired all the time.

- **Humor.** Gradually, the newcomers work toward resolution of their feelings, and their sense of being torn between the new and the old. They begin to accept their new home. They begin to find friends, discover that there are good things about where they are living, and adjust to their lives by coming to terms with both the old and the new ways of living. This is a long process, fraught with feelings of great anxiety in some, because to many, accepting the new means rejecting the old.

- **Home.** Finally, the newcomers become "native" in the sense that where they live is their home and they accept that they are here to stay. This last stage may be years in coming, and for some will never take place.

Thus, what is happening in students' minds and hearts as a result of the drastic changes in their lives has a direct influence on their ability to cope with life and succeed in school.

BEHAVIOR IN THE CLASSROOM

How your students cope with the emotional upheaval in their lives is often reflected in their behavior in class. The affective factors discussed above greatly influence their adjustment. Some students can make the transition from one culture to another with relative ease. Keiko, for instance, was a happy, sunny-tempered girl who liked everybody. It didn't matter to her whether she could speak good English or not; she jumped right into games, discussions, and activities, making the most of the little bit of English she had. Kim used his prowess at soccer to win him friends. Because he was a good player, as well as a congenial, outgoing child, everybody liked him, and he slipped smoothly into his new life in North America.

Other students react to the upheaval with hostility, and act out their aggression, rejecting anything constructive the teachers plan. Yoichiro, for example, managed to make life miserable for everyone, talking loudly in Japanese to his friends, crawling under tables while the teacher was trying to lead a lesson, picking fights, ignoring all instructions as if he didn't understand (even though his teachers knew he did), and refusing to respond to anyone but the Japanese aide.

Other students react with passive-aggressive behavior and selectively decline to participate in activities. For instance, Mary taught a group of students who were upset that they had been transferred to her class, having to leave their teacher of six months. These students were refugees who were brand new to this country and had little control over any facet of their lives. They were comfortable with the teacher they had, and when the system demanded they move up a level to a different teacher, they withdrew. No matter what Mary did for the first few weeks, no matter what adjustments she made to accommodate different levels of abilities, most of the students declined to participate. It was apparent that they were making an attempt to control something in their own lives, and only gradually did they begin to relax and take part in activities.

Some students choose to withdraw completely, effectively shutting out anyone or anything that represents the new culture. Adi withdrew into her lonely self, spending most of her time complaining how unlike North America and Israel were. She never made friends and continued to be unhappy through all her years at high school.

All these factors add up to a myriad of forces that are at work within the learner. Upon reviewing these variables, it may seem an impossible task to help some newcomers learn our language. However, what you do as a teacher is critical to their success, and there are many positive things you can do to assist in making their adjustment to this country (or in the case of Native Americans, to their new environment) and to the English language successful.

Input—The Teacher

Although language is not necessarily taught, it is not enough to assume that, given enough time, students will just "pick it up" on their own. Conscious and directed input from you is necessary.

There are four major things you can do to maximize learning:

- **Provide comprehensible input**
- **Make the environment as stress-free as possible**
- **Provide numerous opportunities for students to hear and speak the language**
- **Provide a network of support**

PROVIDE PLENTY OF COMPREHENSIBLE INPUT

Comprehensible input comes from the language students are exposed to that they can understand. Your students will only learn when the information you teach is meaningful.

COMMUNICATE EFFECTIVELY

- **Use clear, predictable, guessable teacher talk.** Researchers have noted that the way native-English speakers interact with those who don't speak the language is very similar to the way mothers speak to their infants. When adults or native-English speakers speak to each other, their speech is full of stops, starts, and incomplete phrases. When mothers speak to their children, however, they adjust their speech and talk "motherese." Making similar adjustments in your speech to your ESL students is the most helpful way to speak to them.

- **Talk more slowly.** This means at a relaxed rate, not unnaturally slow. Don't overdo it.

- **Reduce the use of idioms.** Idioms are notoriously "untranslatable," that is, if you try to explain them word for word their meaning is lost. Think of trying to explain such expressions as "off the wall," "out of the blue," "grab a seat," "keep it under your hat," or "give me a ballpark figure."

- **Use the active voice and positive sentences.** The passive voice is much more difficult to understand because students have learned that "the subject of the sentence is the actor." For example: "There will be no homework assignments handed in after January 10" is harder to understand than "You must hand in all homework by January 10."

- **Monitor your sentence length; don't make your sentences too long.** Lengthy and complex sentences are often too hard for students to sort through.

- **Simplify your vocabulary whenever possible.** But this should not include technical vocabulary. Content areas have many technical words that are central to concepts being studied, and you should not substitute these words for simpler ones because the students must know them to grasp the central meaning of the lesson. In other cases, finding simpler synonyms for words can make your speech easier to grasp.

- **Use linguistic cues, or attention getters,** such as "look" or "watch" to direct the students' attention to important points. These signals alert listeners to the fact that you consider those points particularly important.

- **Use key words.** Choose several words that are critical to the current lesson, write them on the board, and use them frequently during the discussion so the students will get exposure in several different contexts. Use phonological cues, such as tone and stress, to emphasize these words and call the students' attention to them.

- **Focus the exchange on the here and now.** Abstract concepts are very difficult to understand or express in limited English.

- **Expand the one- or two-word sentences that students produce.** When a student says, for example, "Book home," you can respond, "Oh, your book is at home. Here, use this one."

Another way to provide comprehensible input is through non-verbal cues. You can accomplish this by doing the following:

OTHER SUGGESTIONS

- **Use plenty of visual cues,** such as concrete objects, charts, maps, pictures, photos, and collages.

- **Act out your material or use gestures to help get your meaning across.** Students can then *see* what you are talking about, which provides them with additional clues to meaning, rather than being solely dependent upon translating everything in their heads. Point, mime, role-play, demonstrate an action. Direct the learners' attention to features of the object you are talking about.

- **Use contextual cues.** Words and sentences are more comprehensible when they are used in a context that is understandable. Concepts, such as larger, smaller, fewer, more, are easily understood when they are demonstrated with real objects (such as coins) rather than simply explained.

- **Use more than one method.** Give assignments and lectures orally as well as by writing them on the board. Show a movie or a filmstrip on the same material as your lecture. Have a hands-on project in addition to reading assignments.

- **Check often for understanding.** Stop to see if your ESL students are comprehending the material. Watch for body language, facial expressions, or signs of frustration that will alert you to whether or not the students are understanding. Simply asking "Do you understand?" is not enough. Many students will not admit they don't understand, either because they are ashamed or because they have been taught that their failure will be a sign of disrespect and an affront to the teacher. They often tell you they understand even when they are completely lost. Find alternative ways to check their comprehension, such as asking them to paraphrase a key point. Encourage them to tell you when they don't understand. Develop signals—such as a little throat-clearing—so that they can alert you without overtly stating so. If you teach in chunks, plan an activity to allow them to demonstrate their understanding in nonverbal ways before you go on to the next section.

- **Allow some "wait time," time for the students to hear, understand, and formulate their responses.** Often students have to translate your thoughts into their own language, then re-translate their answer back into English. Native Americans have a longer wait time in their own language; you might have to wait even longer for them to translate and re-translate.

- **Give feedback**, such as a nod, a frown, or a look of bewilderment, so students know how well they are getting their attempts at communicating across.

SET UP A STRESS-FREE ENVIRONMENT

Students who are relaxed and self-confident learn better and faster. You can help reduce the stress your students are under and nurture self-esteem.

REDUCE STRESS AND NURTURE SELF-ESTEEM

- **Show genuine interest in the students, their language, and their culture.**

- **Make your students feel secure.** Even if you can't speak their language, you can reassure them and demonstrate interest and concern through gestures and tone of voice.

- **Allow them to verbalize in their own language.** Many teachers feel that allowing students to talk in their own language will slow their language growth. Some schools even go to the extent of fining or punishing students for talking in their native languages. However, trying to understand a foreign language—in this case English—for hours at a time is physically and mentally exhausting. Students will often do better if they have some "jell time," time when they are not constantly forced to translate information in their heads. Allowing students time to discuss topics together in their own language can actually facilitate learning, because they can focus solely on the content, and are unimpeded by their lack of fluency in English.

- **Avoid forcing your students to speak.** Research shows that forcing students to respond orally before they are ready is a major cause of poor articulation and grammatical control, as well as stress overload. Your students will talk when they are ready.

- **Accept gestures, pantomime, or drawings whenever possible.** These can often demonstrate whether the students understand the concept involved and relieves them of the stress of trying to articulate their thoughts.

- **Make your students feel that they should never be embarrassed or ashamed of their errors.** Errors are a part of learning anything. If students are given the message that errors are bad, or if they are laughed at because of their mistakes, they will clam up. They will only use forms they are perfectly sure of, thus closing the door to learning new forms through practice. Look at mistakes from an analytical rather than a corrective perspective: use them to tell you what your student needs to learn in the future.

- **Don't correct grammatical or pronunciation errors.** Again, meaning is more important than form. Research has shown that correcting errors has little or no value. Corrections can actually impede progress because: 1) the students are given the message that being correct is more important than what they have to say; and 2) students are distracted from the task at hand—communicating. If the meaning of what the students say is unclear, ask for clarification; otherwise, accept the responses as they are given. Learners start with large issues such as the correct words. As their fluency increases, they will iron out the finer points such as word endings and tenses. *Trust* learners to work these things out. You can model the correct form when you respond.

- **Continually reinforce the students' progress.** Keep charts, save their early papers in cumulative folders; show them how far they've come: "This is where you were; this is where you are now. These are the words you've learned."

- **Encourage your students to share their backgrounds and cultures.** ESL students often long to talk about their homelands and cultures and are seldom given this opportunity. For example, asking students to speak about their homelands—perhaps during geography or history lessons—not only provides them with the chance to talk about their countries, but also to use English, speaking about topics familiar to them. And other students in your class will benefit from immediate exposure to a variety of cultures. A welcome by-product is that allowing students to ask questions about the various cultures can help prevent or reduce friction that might be building in the school, because a forum is provided for an open discussion of sensitive topics.

MAXIMIZE STUDENTS' EXPOSURE TO NATURAL COMMUNICATION

The best language learning comes from students' genuine attempts to communicate. Encourage your students' participation in activities within and beyond the classroom.

ENCOURAGE PARTICIPATION

■ **Promote friendships.** You can help promote friendships by introducing students to others who share their interests; by encouraging the student in the class who love to "parent" to take up the cause of the ESL student; by putting together two lonely shy kids; and by prevailing upon all members of the class to be extra sensitive and friendly. As a teacher, your time and energies are limited. You cannot possibly provide students with all the educational input they require as well as meet their social and emotional needs. Everyone wants to have friends and be liked. By promoting friendships you are

❑ Easing the transition for lonely, often heartsick students.

❑ Providing the students with the kind of social relationships in which "getting along" is the most important issue, and learning the language is part and parcel of being a friend. They learn the vocabulary and grammar that is important and useful, while getting feedback that is essential for refining their new language. Put them in "play" situations, whether this involves playing in the sandbox or on the playground (at the elementary level), or competing in friendly games (at any level).

■ **Integrate the ESL students within the classroom.** Make them feel a part of the group. Give them duties, perhaps with another student, such as cleaning erasers or feeding the fish (at the elementary level), or turning in roll sheets or checking equipment (in upper grades).

■ **Make cooperative learning an important part of every class.** Students do not need to work alone to become independent learners. Cooperative learning is a strategy in which a small group of students is involved in an activity or project with a common purpose. Cooperative learning is much more than simply lumping students into a group to work together; often when students are grouped without any ground rules, one or two carry the weight of the assignment.

For effective learning, both groups and tasks must be carefully structured. Cooperative learning involves task specialization within teams; the task cannot be completed without important input from each team member. Heterogeneous grouping, in which one or more ESL students may be in each group, is an important part of cooperative learning. Research has shown that all students—both English speakers and non-English speakers—make substantial gains in their command of the subject. Students get feedback on their attempts to represent problems, have background knowledge supplied by native-English speakers, and profit from discussing problems and observing others' thought processes in tackling issues. Cooperative effort is particularly relevant to some cultures that stress working for the common good as opposed to striving for individual recognition.

YOUR ROLE AS TEACHER

We cannot overstate the importance of your role as teacher. You are on the front line, helping these students make the difficult transition from one culture to another. Often you spend more time with them than their parents do, and can see changes or behavior that family members can not (or do not) recognize.

- **Your most appropriate role is to teach ESL students English, to give them a means to become functional members of the community.**

- **You are also a model of appropriate behavior.** Many of them have lost the leadership of their parents because immigrant or refugee parents are often confused and baffled by our culture, thus cannot effectively interpret society and culture for their children as most parents do. By modeling correct behavior and setting limits, you are making it possible for them to learn how to act in ways we consider acceptable.

- **Adopt a policy of "a little more."** Take the initiative in trying to understand your students, to be aware of the problems they face and the adjustments they're making. A little extra time invested in finding friends for these students, observing how they act and react, and making sure they understand what is expected of them can make the difference between success and failure.

- **Learn a little more.** All Southeast Asians are not alike, just as all Native Americans, Europeans, or Africans are not alike. Ongoing wars and political unrest have divided regions for decades, and

TEACHERS SHOULD...

the memories of violence on both sides creates tensions that transcend country boundaries. Some ethnic groups are very class conscious among themselves and will not associate with those they feel are inferior. Culture, religion, and family patterns all influence your students profoundly. By learning about these, you can be wary of the pitfalls, and be better prepared to understand why and how your students perceive the world. This puts you in a position to modify your classroom to meet the needs of all the students in the class.

- **Be aware of the danger signals.** ESL students fall into the category of "fragile" learners. Fragile learners aren't necessarily those from low income or single-parent families, although these circumstances can be part of newcomers' situations; the fragility refers to the many stresses, traumas, and concerns beyond the students' control, which assault their senses and drain attention and energy. Overcome with feelings of loss and emotional anguish, your students are often "in crisis." Knowing the stages of grief and loss—shock, denial, anger, depression, bargaining, and finally acceptance—as well as being aware of inappropriate behavior—such as laughing at sad stories, crying at a joke, being extremely irritable or suspicious—will help you see beyond the students' behavior and look for causes rather than focusing on the effect and instantly judging or blaming.

- **Learn about resources within the community.** Depression among refugees is very high. Knowing who to turn to when you spot danger signals or behavior problems can relieve untold stress in your students' lives, as well as make your own life easier. Recognize that you are an important member of a team. There are many agencies to help immigrants and refugees. Find out which ones are operating in your area so that you can turn to them when your students need counseling, answers to questions, or help wading through the mire of bureaucracy.

- **Keep the lines of communication open; be a listening ear.** Some of our students have lived through horrors we can't begin to imagine: perhaps seeing their parents blown apart in mine fields, or family members tortured, raped, and murdered by the enemy. The burden of their memories is always with them. Don't probe or openly ask them about their past. Someday something—a smell, a word, a picture—may trigger the memory and they may "tell their story." When that happens, don't try to stop them; it is important to allow your students to share this memory. (Use your discretion as to whether or not it's appropriate for the rest of the class to hear.) Your place is simply to listen and to validate the memory. Let them maintain power by authoring their own story. But then steer them to a professional who can help them in their healing process; it takes a trained professional to help them along the difficult, complicated road to wholeness.

COPING WITH MISBEHAVIOR

Discipline can be difficult and time-consuming when your students can't understand what you are trying to say.

Ideally, you should do as much as you can to prevent misbehavior before it happens. Both children and parents from other cultures may benefit from a sensitive introduction to the student-centered approach to discipline, i.e., leaving the students' integrity and self-worth intact, as opposed to the more traditional punitive approach to discipline that they may be accustomed to. Make your classroom rules very clear. Explain them well, using an interpreter if possible. So much of what we consider acceptable behavior is implicitly understood by North Americans, and yet is not necessarily clear to those from other countries. For instance, one classroom's rules were "1) students will respect all school rules, and 2) students will use acceptable language." Those of us who have grown up in North American schools will know what these rules mean. But those who are coming from a different culture may not. They hear their classmates swearing all the time. How are they supposed to know that this is not acceptable within a teacher's hearing? Unless the rules are explained to them, how will they know what "respecting" the rules means?

We also have to be sure that the consequences for misbehavior are explained to the students.

One teacher we interviewed told us she had kept a student in through lunch time because he had incessantly talked out loud to another student. The teacher used the method of discipline that gives the student warnings by putting check marks on the board. When the student accumulated five check marks, he was kept in during lunch break. She later found out that the student did not understand this discipline method. He did not know that his talking was disruptive to her, or that the check marks on the board were meant for him. Ultimately, she found out that he did not even understand why she had kept him in class while the other students were allowed to go to lunch.

If you have students who are acting up, the first place to start is by reviewing the following:

WHEN THINGS GO WRONG

- **The physical setting.** Where are your students seated? Can they hear, see, observe properly? Do they need the support of students of the same background? (Or do they need to be separated from these students?)

- **The amount of contact for feedback, clarification, and so on.** Are the students aware of what you want them to do? Do they know how to go about doing it? Do they have opportunities to work with you one-on-one? Can they ask questions and get the answers they need to do the work?

- **Your level of expectation.** Was your assessment of your students' abilities accurate or are they getting frustrated?

- **Problems with assignments.** Are they overwhelmed because the assignment is too complex, or have you broken it down in components with each part containing a clearly stated objective?

- **Students' emotional states.** Are you beginning to see some of the danger signals—inappropriate behavior, aggression, withdrawal, or apathy?

- **Cultural mismatch.** It may be, for instance, that some students come from cultures where classes are tightly structured. In our less formal classes, students may be unable to figure out what rules are in effect and how they should behave. They may be frustrated at the contradiction between those behaviors they believe are acceptable and your behavioral expectations.

If no problems exist in your setup, and you don't believe culture is a factor, then confront students individually with the problems. Communication may be difficult, so try to get the help of a translator. A student may be able to recognize that problems exist and may even be able to tell you what would improve the situation. For example, he might be able to say, "You talk too fast and then I don't understand how to do the assignment. Could you write it on the board?"

More likely, however, the student will deny that any problems exist. He may even react with hostility and end up blaming you for all his problems, or he may withdraw and say very little to enlighten you.

RESOLVING BEHAVIOR PROBLEMS

Working through the following steps can help resolve behavior problems, because in the end the student will know exactly what is expected of him.

1. **Review what the correct behavior is.**

2. **State clearly what he can and cannot do, using language that he can understand.** For instance, "Stay in your seat when I am talking. No crawling under tables," or "No sharing of answers." While we want to be positive and provide positive models of behavior, the word *No* clearly sets the parameters of what is acceptable and what isn't.

3. **Avoid putting yourself in a position that you can't change later,** such as stating unequivocally that all plagiarism will be awarded with instant failure. Your student may not have any idea what the word plagiarism means, thus may not understand that copying directly from a book or his classmate's essay is wrong.

4. **Tell the student how he can correct the problem.** If he is in high school and has the language capabilities, he may even be able to plan strategies for correcting the problem himself.

5. **Detail the consequences if the student does not comply with the resolutions you have established.** Be flexible. Be prepared to negotiate, but hold on to reasonable standards.

Grading Suggestions

Grading ESL students is another difficult issue. How can you grade students whose language interferes with their ability to compete with their English-speaking classmates? Your students may be outstanding, and yet, hampered by their lack of proficiency with the language, they may be unable to display what they are actually capable of. According to your needs, you can adapt the following suggestions for grading:

- Don't grade at all until these new students have had a chance to catch on.

- For elementary students: Modify the vocabulary list given in Appendix C and ditto it off as a "report card" for parents, to demonstrate what their children have learned.

- For upper levels: If your school requires you to give a grade, consider giving an "incomplete" for the first marking period.

- If students have met the criteria or minimum competencies established for that marking period, give passing grades.

Conclusion

Dealing with students from different backgrounds entails much planning and research on your part. However, the benefits in terms of the enrichment each newcomer brings to your class far outweigh the negatives. By creating plenty of opportunities for interaction, providing appropriate feedback, and being sensitive to the types of changes your students are coping with, you can set up the optimal environment for learning.

WHOLE LANGUAGE LEARNING AND THE FOUR SKILLS

In this chapter, we will discuss the "whole language" approach to learning and its importance for second language learners. We will focus on

- Using the whole language approach with ESL students

- Literacy as every teacher's responsibility

- Strategies for promoting the acquisition of literacy skills

The Whole Language Approach to Teaching/Learning

In the last several years the move toward integrating the language arts—the "whole language" approach to teaching/learning—has gained widespread credence. Research has shown that reading, writing, speaking, and listening are all parts of students' general development and should not be viewed as discrete skills that can be taught in isolation. With the whole language approach, learning is not divorced from meaning and divided into separate activities such as penmanship, phonics, or spelling; nor is there the artificial separation of reading from writing and discussion. Rather, the focus is on "meaning-making" by readers, writers, speakers, and listeners, all within the context of real communication.

What this means for every teacher, including those with second language learners in their class, is that

Opportunities for reading, writing, speaking, and listening must be "real." Real situations—reading to enjoy a story or to find out how to fix a bike, writing a letter to complain about a canceled TV show—are intrinsically motivating because they have purpose. ESL students often pass driver's education with flying colors in a remarkably short time. They learn to read the driving manuals and

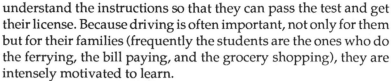

understand the instructions so that they can pass the test and get their license. Because driving is often important, not only for them but for their families (frequently the students are the ones who do the ferrying, the bill paying, and the grocery shopping), they are intensely motivated to learn.

The situations must be meaningful, i.e., meaning-full. We communicate in order to accomplish something: to learn, to have our needs met, to get along with other people, or just to play. We have a purpose and an audience. Infants do not learn to talk by learning that we put the subject before the verb or add *s* to nouns to make them plural. They learn words like *bye bye*, *juice*, and *milk* within contexts that have meaning to them. We must provide second-language learners with the same kinds of opportunities so that they can make sense of language by using it for purposes that have relevance to them. Often the tasks students are given are phony exercises: tracing and copying the letters of the alphabet again and again; learning lists of words simply because they all begin with the same sound or demonstrate a phonics principle; punctuating sentences that someone else has written; listing all the nouns in a paragraph; repeating two sounds until they can hear the difference. These exercises have fractionated learning into little bits and pieces that, while important components of the reading, writing, speaking, and listening processes, of themselves make little sense to the learner. "Whole texts," not just isolated words or sentences, but poems, newspaper articles, novels, textbooks, letters, comic books, grocery lists, and songs all provide meaning in meaningful contexts.

The learning situations must be also be integrated so that all four skills are used together. Rather than simply discussing a topic—whether it be about what they saw at the zoo yesterday or the legalization of drugs—students can write (or have you write) what they know and think, discuss what they have written, and further their understanding of the event or issue by listening to each other's thoughts and interpretations. Then they can capitalize on what they have learned orally by using their newly learned vocabulary in their reading, writing, and sharing.

Literacy In and Beyond the Language Arts Classroom

Fortunately, most school boards and administrations recognize that helping students achieve literacy is not solely the job of the elementary teacher or the high school English teacher, it is the job of *all* teachers, from the art teacher to the phys. ed. instructor, from the band director to the shop teacher. Reading and writing are an integral part of every course within the curriculum, from math to driver education. Language instruction is everybody's business.

Literacy is not simply the ability to read and write, it is much more than that: it is the ability to use one's reading and writing skills to participate efficiently and effectively in today's society.

SECOND-LANGUAGE LITERACY

Second-language learners are not alike. They come to us with vast differences in their background knowledge and experience with print. Some come from countries with a high literacy rate where they learned to read in their own language; others are from cultures that have no written language, and therefore have no reading skills to transfer to the task of reading in English. It's not enough to simply label a non-reader "illiterate," because different types of illiteracy demand different strategies.

Of those who cannot read English, Haynes and Haverson (1982) distinguish four types:

❑ **Preliterates.** These are learners who speak a language for which there is no written form. They have grown up in villages where there are no books, signs, or magazines. They often have no idea that those squiggles on the page, which we call print, are supposed to have meaning.

❑ **Non-literates.** These learners speak a language for which there *is* a written form that uses the alphabet, but they have not learned to read. They know that reading and writing have a purpose and that those marks have meaning, but they have simply not learned these skills.

❑ **Semi-literates.** These students have the very basic skills of literacy, such as knowing how to write their names, but not much more than that.

❑ **Non-alphabetics.** These are literate learners from countries that do not have alphabetic language. Logographic systems, such as Chinese, and syllabic systems, such as Japanese, use characters that represent complete words or syllables instead of individual letters as we have in English. These learners have learned the skills of reading and need to transfer them to the new language, but don't need to start again from the very beginning, squiggles-are-words stage.

For those ESL students who are literate in their own language, do not delay reading and writing until they have acquired advanced listening skills and oral fluency.

FOUR TYPES OF PEOPLE WHO CANNOT READ ENGLISH

Much of the research in second-language acquisition has compared it to first-language acquisition. There are many parallels; thus many teachers, both classroom and ESL, adhere to the following acquisition model:

LISTENING > SPEAKING > READING > WRITING

First-language learners, of course, follow this pattern, spending their first year or so listening to the language around them, then speaking, and only later learning to read and write. It seems natural to apply this model to second-language learners; many of our students do progress through these stages. And anyone who has tried to learn a second language knows how much easier it is to understand the language than to speak it. However, this listening-speaking-reading-writing model presents some very serious problems that need to be addressed.

Many of our ESL students have studied English in schools in their native countries. They have often been taught by other non-native English speakers and have spent a good deal of time learning English grammar. They may know how to read and write in our language, but cannot speak or make themselves understood. The listening-speaking-reading-writing model ignores their strengths by pushing them to learn to speak and listen before they are given reading and writing tasks.

Teachers who follow this model adhere rigidly to the belief that oral skills must be taught before reading and writing. Much compelling research demonstrates otherwise. Hudelson (1983), Edelsky (1985), and Ammon (1985), for instance, have shown that students who are limited in their speaking ability can still compose texts and learn to read. Learning to read and write should go hand in hand with learning to speak. While learners must have a core vocabulary to start reading, to delay reading and writing until students have oral fluency is to substantially delay their ability to function in the regular classroom. Therefore, while working on the oral skills, it is also critical to introduce print within meaningful contexts.

Pre- and non-literate students often, on the other hand, need a year or more of simple exposure to print before they can actually begin reading. Teachers frequently get frustrated because these students don't seem to be learning. But learning to read is a slow process, and students must first be allowed the time to get the exposure to print they require.

WHERE TO BEGIN

The first step in learning to read and write in the new language is learning words that are useful to the learners, usually the first words they have learned to speak in their first language. The strategies that follow provide a bridge to the reading and writing tasks required of students, both literate and non-literate. These strategies do not necessitate the overt teaching of reading and writing skills, but are simply examples of ways to promote literacy in any classroom. These are the types of activities that can provide meaningful, quality instruction to groups of students working at widely varying levels of language proficiency. This is not an exhaustive list, but should help you validate the fact that many of the activities that you are already doing with your English-speaking students are also appropriate for your ESL students. This list should also help you develop your own methods and materials. These strategies can be used with the class as a whole or with individual ESL students. The activities are "rich" activities because students at different levels of ability and competence can profit from them. Many of these strategies help you to create a "print rich environment." This is the first priority in any classroom, particularly one that contains ESL students. In order to establish the speech–print connection, students need to see words in use, in action.

SURROUNDING STUDENTS WITH WORDS—SOME STRATEGIES

- **Label items in the classroom.** Label such things as the window, cupboard, desk. Learning the English words for objects they already know in their first language is one of the first ways students learn a second language; therefore it makes sense to put written labels on these objects immediately. If they are already literate, they can also write labels for each item in their first language.

    To reinforce visual discrimination and practice sight word recognition, make labeling into a game. Label classroom items, then make a duplicate set of labels and ask the student to match them to the labels about the room. This activity is appropriate for all age levels and classes, especially in content areas such as science and physical education, which have their own specialized vocabulary and equipment. Labeling is particularly useful when you have new students and must find worthwhile tasks to occupy them while they adjust to their new environment.

    After you, an aide, or a buddy have played this with a student a number of times, take the labels off the items and have the student return as many labels as he or she knows to their proper places.

- **Make and display charts.** Whenever possible, combine a word with a picture. Display charts that combine words and illustrations. Attractive easy-to-use charts are available ready-made from most teacher supply stores, or ESL students can be given the task of making the charts, thus reinforcing the word meanings as well as allowing them to contribute in non-verbal ways to the class. Some suggestions for chart construction:

Elementary level

❏ Colors, animals, money, toys, shapes

All levels

❏ Science: the human body, food chains, ecosystems

❏ Math: symbols such as > < + = % with their verbal meanings. Words for equivalents such as: *sum = add difference = subtract*

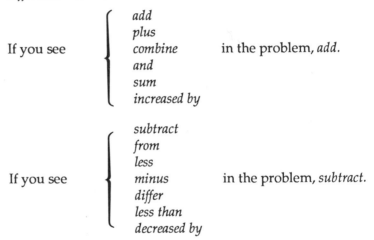

If you see { add / plus / combine / and / sum / increased by } in the problem, *add.*

If you see { subtract / from / less / minus / differ / less than / decreased by } in the problem, *subtract.*

❏ Phys. ed.: equipment; familiar commands or techniques, such as dribbling, passing; common vocabulary

❏ Music: time equivalent for notes; words for symbols such as *treble* and *bass clef*

❏ Social studies: maps; time lines

❏ Shop: safety rules; equipment and tools

■ **Display lists.** Display lists of words that the class has brainstormed as a lead-in to a writing exercise, unit of study, or activity.

All levels

❏ Appropriate behavior in the classroom

❏ Phys ed.: the rules of games

❏ Science: important vocabulary; lab rules and procedures

- Math: technical vocabulary; words with specific math meanings, such as *product* or *square*

- Art: rules for set-up and clean-up

- Social science: vocabulary for current unit of study

- Language arts: color words; emotions; winter words; vivid verbs; story starters such as *firsts, lasts, important people, things I get mad about*

- **Design activities using environmental print.** You can invent a host of activities that employ words seen in everyday life, such as McDonald's, Safeway, Stop. Because these words are relevant, most children know them long before they come to kindergarten, and even the slowest learners or the newest ESL students can pick out words they recognize. Many of the words are intimately tied to a configuration or logo that gives a decoding clue. McDonald's, for instance, is written with the "golden arches"; *Stop* is always within the context of a red octagon. As the students develop more skills, they will be able to decode the words without the use of these visual clues, but they are an important first step in equating sign-symbol correspondence.

Elementary level

- Have children bring in empty boxes and cans and put together a class grocery store.

- Have the students brainstorm all the places they see words: labels, billboards, television, packages, traffic signs, and so on.

- With the entire class, take a tour of the school or the neighborhood to scout for words.

All levels

- Have students collect all the words they see and categorize them in different ways.

- Have students keep three-day journals of all the different kinds of reading they do in a day, from street signs to school assignments.

- Have a T-shirt design contest.

- Write a class yearbook.

- Write a classroom telephone directory.

- **Use I-can-read books and dictionaries.** The variations on this theme are endless at all levels. This is another way to reinforce

students' vocabulary and demonstrate what your regular students know; it is also an activity you can implement immediately with your new students.

- Beginning students can cut pictures from magazines or newspapers of all the words they recognize, from *house* to *lion*, then paste one picture onto each page of a blank book. Underneath each picture, you or an aide print "I can read..." and then the word. Usually the students quickly remember that each page starts with "I can read" and, since they chose the pictures, they are able to "read" the book almost immediately and feel a real sense of achievement.

- Preliterate students can cut out pictures of things for which they know the English word, and paste the pictures into their books. In the content areas, you can implement this activity before students are able to do regular class work.

- Students can categorize words—foods, body parts, furniture, for example—and add new words to each category as they expand their vocabulary.

- Those who are already literate and have learned more English can print the words next to their pictures. Advanced students can alphabetize and write definitions for their words.

- ESL students can work with an aide or a buddy, using their dictionary for review. They can also practice the words by themselves while the rest of the class is involved in other activities. This is a terrific confidence booster; it demonstrates concretely to students how far they have advanced in their knowledge of English.

- **Use games.** For rainy days or Friday afternoons, stock up on games. These are not simply time fillers; treat them seriously. Games provide a context for socializing and reinforcing language. The game Sorry, for instance, uses colors, counting, recognizing numbers, and several important survival words, such as *sorry* and *start*. Learning the rules to the game requires careful listening. Games have a clear repetitive structure, in which words are tied closely to actions. They are also strong motivators. Even the shyest, most reluctant, or non-verbal ESL student will get involved in a game and forget his inhibitions. When the focus is on having fun, vocabulary is learned as a by-product, but it *is* learned and students don't forget. Here are some suggestions:

  - Board games: Sorry, The Last Straw, Candyland, Operation, Bingo, Hungry Hippo, Yahtzee, Clue

- For older students: Monopoly, Risk, Boggle, Scrabble

- Guessing games: Simon Says; Mother May I?; Win, Lose, or Draw

- Card games: Concentration, War, Old Maid, Go Fish, Cribbage

- Word games: Twenty Questions, Ghost

- Many games can be modified, with questions tailored for any content class or lesson. Make your own version of Trivial Pursuit, Jeopardy, or Go Fish.

- **Use tapes.** You can tape almost anything—stories, songs, rhymes, or chants. Tapes are useful: they reinforce the speech-to-print connection as well as meaningful vocabulary, and allow your ESL students to work on reading while you are engaged in another activity. However, tapes should not be used simply as fillers when you have nothing else for these students to do. Taped books used by ESL students should already be familiar to them, having been read and discussed with the class or another student. You should not try to "break new ground" with tapes; they are better used as reinforcement of previously covered material. For beginning students, be sure to program in a "beep" at each page-ending so they know when to turn the page. Without this you can sometimes discover a student "reading" three pages behind the text!

  - You get double benefits if you allow your regular students to do the taping for you, giving them extra practice in reading.

  - Tape songs for pleasure listening. Try to include English-word recordings of songs from students' own cultures.

  - If possible, send tapes home with the children. Discussions with parents in their own language will benefit students greatly.

  - At the secondary level, tape your lectures so that the students can take them home and listen to them a second time for learning reinforcement.

- **Use drama.** Drama is one of the most effective ways to use the four skills and to help students articulate and demonstrate what they know; the students consolidate the material you've presented by using it in a "real" situation, and practice their language skills by generating their own dialogue. In any class you—or the students—can write a short play about a theme you are working on. If possible, videotape the plays.

- History: Dramatize an important historical event.

- Government: Enact a bill into law; hold a trial; poll the student body on an issue; hold an election.

- Social Sciences: Use socio-dramas—set up a situation in which the students have to make difficult choices and ad-lib their solutions.

- English: Re-enact a scene from a play or a piece of literature.

- Elementary: Use rhymes, fairy tales, and puppet shows. Puppet shows are particularly effective for ESL learners when they manipulate the puppets while you read the script. The students are responsible for understanding the material and responding on cue, but are not required to produce language themselves.

■ **Use patterned language.** The writers of those endless drill-and-practice foreign-language textbooks recognized the importance of patterned language in language learning. Patterned language has many positive features:

- The repetition gives students the practice they need in order to internalize a form.

- Students can use these patterns as building blocks—they make generalizations from the patterns they have learned, and can then move on to create their own sentences.

- When the forms are practiced consistently, they become instinctive. Students can focus on communication and learning new structures with the security of having a few forms well learned.

Linda Ventriglia, author of *Conversations of Miguel and Maria* (1985), notes that students learning a second language naturally adopt a strategy of following patterns, but they learn patterns that are *meaningful* and *useful* to them, ones that can be applied in a social context. Long meaningless drills found in textbooks are easily forgotten. But by selecting topics that interest the learners, using phrases elicited from them, and practicing these phrases in a game-like situation, you can use patterns successfully, not only to reinforce vocabulary, but to introduce new linguistic patterns in a systematic way. The students can easily transfer the patterns they have learned and apply them to new social contexts.

Therefore, make a distinction between these types of sentences and the traditional "This is a..." sentences found in many older texts in which students simply fill in blanks. Barb once consulted with a tutor who had been working on such sentences with two twelve-year-old boys. They couldn't remember the difference between *a* and *an* from one day to the next, and the tutor had decided that they were learning disabled. Jumping to this conclusion based upon such insufficient data was damaging. The boys weren't learning disabled, they were simply bored struggling with a very minor grammatical point that had little relevance or significance to them in the face of the huge task of learning the English language.

You can avoid tedium, while retaining the positive aspects of this type of continued practice of forms, with the following types of patterned language.

TYPES OF PATTERNED LANGUAGE

- **Songs.** Songs can be a delightful way to work on rhythm, pronunciation, and vocabulary. People of all ages love to learn and sing songs. You can ask your native-English-speaking students to find pictures or props to teach ESL students the words.

  The use of songs doesn't have to be limited to the primary grades, and the songs don't have to be juvenile tunes only a kindergartner would love. Students of all ages listen to the Top 40, whether they understand the words or not, and many second-language learners comment that they learn a great deal of their language from the radio and TV. You can capitalize on this by bringing in songs for discussion, songs to illustrate a theme or even a grammatical point. Use such perennial favorites as Bob Dylan or Peter, Paul, and Mary, or social commentators like Pink Floyd, or language-development songwriters/artists such as Bob Schneider of Toronto. Give students copies of the lyrics so that they can read them as they follow along. If you can't stand to watch MTV or Much Music, get one of your students to tape some of the more interesting songs for class discussion.

  - History: use folk songs or spirituals such as "Swing Low Sweet Chariot" to enliven an understanding of slavery.

  - Social Science: use songs from other lands to give insight into other cultures.

  - Government: use protest songs such as "Eve of Destruction," "Rain on the Scarecrow," or Neil Sedaka's "The Immigrant."

  - English: English classes are the perfect place to study songs. You can look at poetic theme, rhyme, sense of place, as well as natural rhythm and cadence. The early Beatles' and Rolling Stones' ballads are naturals, as are some by contemporaries such as Peter Gabriel and Kate Bush. It may be dangerous to allow students to choose their own, since many rock groups like Aerosmith and rappers like The 2 Live Crew write a wide range of songs that sometimes includes erotic or violent material. You may want to get together with other teachers and compile a list of songs you would like to include and let the students choose from these. Or have the students copy the lyrics and get prior approval for a song to study.

- **Chants.** Chants are another form of patterned language. Good sources for chants are *Jazz Chants* and *Jazz Chants for Children* by Carolyn Graham, a collection of chants (with accompanying cassette) designed for ESL learners, but just as much fun for other children—and adults. The teacher's guide offers suggestions for presenting the chants, and for incorporating everything from actions to reading and writing. But the bottom line is that they're fun—for the student and for you. If, along the way, your ESL students learn a point of grammar or a North American idiom, so much the better. For the junior and senior high levels you can use pep rally chants.

- **Frame sentences.** What if the elementary curriculum guide mandates that you teach your students such words as *can, run, jump, I, and, the, go,* and *was* by October? Or suppose your tenth grader says things like, "I didn't brought my homework," or "I seed that movie last week." Is there any alternative to relying solely on a basal reader or simple memorization of word lists?

One particularly effective use of patterned language involves frame sentences, developed by Marlene and Robert McCracken (1979), which allow the teacher to plug student ideas into a controlled pattern of words. For example:

What can you do with your feet?
> I can walk with my feet.
> I can run with my feet.

What else can walk?
> A dog can walk.
> A horse can walk.
> An elephant can walk (and so on)

What can't walk?
> A fish can't walk.
> A worm can't walk (and so on)

Where can you walk?
> I can walk to...
> I can walk on...
> I can walk over...
> I can walk through...
> I can walk around...

All levels

The McCrackens recommend spending at least one to five days on each frame used. They also stress quantity, and insist that, for proper reinforcement, the teacher elicit thirty to forty (or more) brainstormed responses for each frame. Every day students can chant back the previous day's frames and even brainstorm new responses.

Elementary levels

Use frame sentences to help students understand difficult material or to elicit what they already know about a topic. Ask the question, "What do you know about...?" For instance, "What do you know about mammals?" Set up the frame sentence, "A mammal is an animal that has..." Any topic or issue can be introduced this way.

Frames can be derived from basal readers, from content-area units being studied, from virtually any source. Once you get started using frame sentences, the possibilities are endless.

With ESL students this is a particularly effective way to work on a problem once you've diagnosed a need. For instance, if the student needs to work on the irregular past tense, you can begin sentences like:

Yesterday I went...
Yesterday I saw...
Yesterday I ate...

Or you can teach conjunctions and transition words that ESL students often find difficult:

A horse can walk and so can an elephant.
A horse can walk but a fish can't.
A worm can't walk and neither can a fish.

- **Rhymes.** Small children enjoy rhymes, often repeating them over and over again to themselves. Non-native-English speakers can pick them up very quickly and derive great pleasure and a sense of achievement from being able to recite them. Rhymes expose and allow ESL students to practice (within the context of a whole text) the forty-four sounds of English. Learners are able to model intonation, stress, and pronunciation in a fun, dynamic, and meaningful way.

  Rhymes can also be incorporated into whole language activities at the elementary level.

  ❑ Choose a familiar rhyme such as Humpty Dumpty. Using pictures for each scene, have the students put them in order. When they have learned the words and the sequence of the rhyme, they can begin to match pictures with words.

  ❑ Prepare a pocket chart of word cards so that the students can follow the words as they chant them. Make duplicate word cards of the rhymes, and then have the ESL students place them in the correct order as they recite. Beginners can start by matching word cards and placing them on top of the words of the poem that has been written on large paper. This not only reinforces the sound-to-print connection, but builds sight-word vocabulary.

  ❑ Say a word and have the group find it on the chart. Remove several words and have individuals replace them in the proper sequence, chanting the rhyme to check if the words have been replaced properly.

  ❑ Have class members make their own books into which they can copy the rhymes and illustrate them. This reinforces, in an enjoyable way, not only reading, but writing and spelling too.

- Give a rhymes concert.
- Act the rhymes out.
- Have students tape themselves reciting the rhymes. Include ESL students taping some they have learned well. Have them tape on several different occasions so that they can monitor their own progress when they hear their voices played back.

Sourcebooks for activities based on rhymes are available in most teacher supply stores.

Conclusion

With language learning, the key is authenticity—using whole language, rather than fractionating reading, writing, listening, and speaking into separate skills, then breaking them down even further into meaningless exercises.

Whole language activities give you options that you can incorporate into the themes you are working on. They don't involve a lot of extra planning or extra work, but the benefits you reap in terms of your students' language acquisition are great.

I wish I have a nice mother
and I wish my sister and my brother are nice
to me
I wish I have a bird.
I wish I have a best friend like my sister
does
I wish I have a nice bike like my sister
does.
I wish I have a lot of picture in my bedroom
and I wish I have a nice day
I wish I always be with my friend
I wish I always going up to the mothing

READING

5

In this chapter, we will discuss the basics for teaching and promoting reading with ESL students. We will focus on

- ❑ Ways of promoting success in reading
- ❑ Choosing and developing reading materials
- ❑ Meeting the particular reading needs of your students
- ❑ Helping develop reading skills in the language arts and the content areas.

Lee could not read. She had come from Laos at sixteen with no previous schooling and had been in school in North America for two years. She could speak very well, and could even write a bit, but she still had not learned to read. She was now eighteen and school officials were telling her that they had done all they could and that this was her last year; whether she graduated or not, she had to go. The ESL teacher turned her over to the latest in a string of tutors and told the tutor to work on phonics. It hadn't worked before, but, as the teacher said, "We've tried everything else."

Lee is not an isolated case. Many students come to our schools and seem to grasp the spoken language immediately, but lag far behind in reading skills. The ways we have traditionally taught North American children to read often do not work with ESL students, and like Lee, these students struggle with the rudiments year after frustrating year. What can be done?

READING AS A WHOLE SKILL

Many component skills make up the act of reading: recognizing letters and words, predicting, and confirming, to name a few. The temptation for teachers of ESL students, particularly those with illiterate students, is to focus on teaching the alphabet and a large sight vocabulary before attempting whole texts. However, with ESL learners, focusing on each skill in isolation can not only be counterproductive, but can result in poor readers or even in those unable to read at all.

For *all* learners, reading must be for meaning. Reading is defined as getting meaning from print; if one is not getting meaning, one is not reading. Before anyone can learn to read, the learner must understand that the language that we hear and speak can be written down, and that, conversely, what we see in written form can say something to us. Therefore, one of the fundamental things students must learn is what reading is and why we read.

The Commission on Reading states in *Becoming a Nation of Readers* (1985) that "the most useful form of practice is doing the whole skill of reading—that is, reading meaningful text for the purpose of understanding the message it contains." We can make the analogy to a jigsaw puzzle—no piece is useful on its own, unconnected to the rest. Only together do all the pieces make a comprehensible whole. There is only one way to learn how to read: by reading. Literacy must be introduced naturally through the use of literature that the students find interesting or entertaining, in an environment where both reading and writing are celebrated and encouraged.

To enable your ESL students to learn to read or to make the transition to reading in English, you must create a balance between making materials available and consciously directing their acquisition of reading skills. Thus, **newcomers need**

- **To be immersed in real reading**

- **A wealth of materials that they will be capable of reading**

- **A helpful guide—someone to guide them in their acquisition of English language skills**

- **An enabling environment**

Immersion—Make Reading a Daily Commitment

Being immersed in reading involves reading a variety of written materials for a variety of purposes: textbooks, magazines, newspapers, recipes, manuals, comic books, TV guides, and so on. Sentences are easier to read than words, paragraphs are easier than sentences, and whole texts the easiest of all, because the text gives clues about the meanings of words and concepts that the student might miss on the first try. Teachers often give beginning readers basal readers, believing that because they are shorter and filled with simple words, they are easier. In actual fact, they are not. Often, for example, series of sentences such as, "See the toy train. See my toy train go," are so vapid and devoid of clues, that if children do not know the word *train* the first time, they will certainly not pick it up with a variation of the sentence.

Immersion also means encountering print throughout the day, with time in each period devoted either solely to reading or to a reading-related task, such as making handicrafts, following written instructions, playing games with written rules, and so on.

In chapter 4, "Whole Language Learning and the Four Skills," we listed many ways to make your classroom a print-rich environment. Here are additional ways to help your students to learn to read or make the transition to reading in English.

MORE STRATEGIES TO HELP CHILDREN LEARN TO READ

The Commission on Reading asserts that reading aloud to children is "...the single most important activity for building the knowledge required for eventual success in reading." Jim Trelease, author and national advocate of reading aloud, takes it one step further. "When teachers take time to read to their class they are not neglecting the curriculum. *Reading IS the curriculum.* [The italics are ours.] The principal ingredient of all learning and teaching is language."

READING ALOUD

This is especially important for ESL students who are either illiterate or insufficiently fluent in English to read on their own. If you have a regular reading time every day in your class, you shouldn't feel that you are wasting the ESL students' time just because they are not able to understand every word. At the very least they see that words have meaning, that writing can be translated into oral speech, and that books are made for knowledge and enjoyment. They are listening to language, listening to others discuss and enjoy what was written. The enjoyment factor should not be dismissed lightly. School is a stressful place for many children, and especially so for ESL students. Being able to sit and relax and simply listen to a story adds pleasure to their day.

Besides the obvious benefits of giving students a chance to hear words in context, to develop listening skills, and to increase vocabulary, reading to students motivates them to want to read more. They become "hooked on books," which many experts contend is the key to reading success.

This does not apply only to the little ones in primary grades who are first learning to read, or to those whose skills are low. Read to all students at all levels. Their ability to understand print often exceeds their ability to decode it. When we were at the one-word stage of language, our parents didn't limit the books they read to us to one-word books. We listened to books far beyond our language capacity, often including many words beyond our understanding. The same holds true for ESL students. Their interests, comprehension, and sophistication may be far above what they are able to read for themselves. By reading to them, you will be extending their exposure to different types of literature as well as increasing their vocabulary and understanding.

Don't stop with stories. In the upper grades, reading demands are different and more difficult. Science, history, and math students in junior and senior high schools are faced with the task of extracting information from texts that presuppose a high level of reading and know-how to find the information they need. In wading through the material to find that information, they may need help. Even in her senior-level linguistics classes, Barb finds that reading parts of texts aloud makes them more accessible to students, because she can explain difficult concepts as she goes along and direct students' attention to what she feels is important in the text.

ONE-ON-ONE READING AND SMALL GROUP READING

By far the best strategy is to read and discuss books one-on-one with your ESL students. You can instantly gauge how much they understand, go over unclear parts, and review vocabulary in a personalized way. As you read, move your finger along under the words, synchronizing speech with print. This helps students perceive the speech–sound correspondence within a relaxed, pleasurable atmosphere. Weak readers and ESL students in particular can benefit from this type of reading. You can turn this activity over to an older or stronger reader, an aide, a parent, or anyone with free time within the school. If you haven't time for one-on-one reading, small groups can also be effective.

CHORAL READING

With choral reading—reading a story in unison—first read the story or other text aloud. Then, with the words available for everybody to see (whether from a big book, a chart, or an overhead) read it again, inviting all the class to read with you. This encourages participation from everyone. Even the poor readers can chime in when they know a word or phrase. In the anonymity of a group, they do not have to know all the words, and aren't put on the spot when they don't. Especially effective are predictable books, such as Bill Martin's *Brown Bear, Brown Bear*, or cumulative stories such as "I Know an Old Lady," "This Is the House that Jack Built," or "The Napping House." Choral reading does not have to be limited to the primary grades; songs, poems, and chants can be used throughout the upper grades too.

SUSTAINED SILENT READING (SSR)

Because reading is a skill that needs practice, an extremely successful way to develop interest and skill in reading is through sustained reading. SSR is a much more effective form of practice than drills in isolated skills. Sustained silent reading should be an integral part of every school day. Devote a certain amount of time to free reading, ranging from just five minutes with kindergarten children, to as much as the whole class period with older or more experienced students. Allow students to select their own reading material to read during that time. No book reports, comprehension questions, or records should be required. The only requirement should be that they read silently from one book for a specified amount of time. Non-English speakers can profit from this time even though they might not yet be able to read any words. Steer your ESL students toward books you have read aloud in class or books that others within the class have written. The best books are those which are familiar, having been read and discussed prior to the ESL students' time alone with them.

One key to success, write Anne Forester and Margaret Reinhard in *The Learners' Way* (1989), is to have a large stock of reading materials available, both new and familiar. Fill your classroom with wordless picture books, catalogs, magazines, trade books, comic books, library books, class- or individually-made books.

The other key is for you to read too. Often SSR fails because the teacher uses this time to grade papers, take roll, or converse with small groups about other school business. This defeats the entire purpose of SSR. It is important for you to read honestly during that time, to model serious reading, and possibly to share what you read after the reading time is up. Many students have never seen an adult reading, and by reading yourself you are conveying the message that reading is important, as well as pleasurable.

SHARING TIME

Build in time for readers to share what they have read. A study of second-language learners by Elley and Mangubhai (in the *Reading Research Quarterly*, 1983) found that when teachers flooded the classroom with books and allowed time for sharing, those children made significantly larger gains in reading than children in classrooms that used only basal readers or limited the reading to SSR— without time for sharing. Students get excited about their friends' choices and are eager to read and share in the experience.

Provide a Wealth of Materials at Your Students' Level

Finding suitable reading materials for non-English speakers can be a problem for many teachers. However, there are ways of gathering and making appropriate materials for each level. These are discussed here.

MAKE BASAL READERS MORE ACCESSIBLE

The problem of suitable reading materials for non-English-speaking students is a major problem for those teachers stuck with an ineffective and old-fashioned series of basal readers or anthologies. (Elementary basal readers can be boring, irrelevant, and condescending to readers; anthologies are filled with stories and poems that someone else liked.) Although many schools and school districts are now moving toward the complete elimination of basals, and a number of publishers are working hard to produce materials that reflect current knowledge of psycholinguistic theory, your school may have invested thousands of dollars in outdated basal readers and anthologies, and have little left over for new reading materials for the many levels of reading ability you might have in your classroom. The only sensible and realistic solution to this dilemma is to live with what you've got and do your best to modify and/or supplement the materials to suit your students. There are several things you can do to make basal readers more accessible to your ESL students.

- **Supplement the basic textbooks** as much as possible with language experience stories (discussed on page 8) and library books.

- **Encourage extensive reading**—which often involves students reading texts at easier levels, but on a wide range of topics.

- **Expose students to the many different types of reading available in the "real" world,** such as magazines, newspapers, cereal boxes, recipes, how-to manuals, as well as expository and persuasive writing, so that they are aware of different styles of text and the need for different ways to read.

DIFFERENT STRATEGIES FOR THE VARYING NEEDS OF YOUR STUDENTS

USE PICTURE BOOKS

Picture books are a good way to introduce reading to all levels of ESL newcomers. Because these books do not depend on text to tell a story, they can be used to stimulate talk and later writing. At first you can allow students to simply page through the books, perhaps during sustained silent reading time. But don't take for granted that they will know even such simple things as holding the book right side up, or starting at the front.

Ask them to identify elements of the illustrations. Then, when the students have acquired more English, you can ask them to tell you the story. You might have them make captions for each page, or you can transcribe their version of the story.

Encourage them to discuss these books in their own language with a peer, an aide, or at home with a parent. In this way they do not have to depend upon their fragmented knowledge of English to talk about what they see in the pictures.

Picture books are important because they help the students develop thinking skills. They challenge them to think about and articulate what they perceive. Read and Smith (1982) have identified other important skills that these books can help develop:

- Sequencing—learning how to distinguish a sequence of pictures and develop vocabulary words such as *first, next, then,* and so on. Narratives in other cultures are often very different from our own; therefore learning "story grammar" is a fundamental skill that should not be taken for granted.

- Identifying the who, what, when, where of the story

- Getting the main idea

- Making inferences

- Predicting what will happen next

- Drawing conclusions

- Establishing cause and effect

Picture books are not only for primary grades. Books such as *Where's Waldo?* are popular at any age, and some of the wonderful illustrations found in the reproductions of old classic storybooks are appropriate for all ages.

At the junior and senior high school levels, in which students may feel condescended to by the use of picture books, you can—with the help of the librarian, the yearbook editor, and some enterprising photography students—make your own library.

MAKE YOUR OWN LIBRARY

- **Start with yearbooks.** If the yearbook teacher has leftover pictures you might make your own classroom yearbook.

- **Make photo albums.** Take Polaroid pictures of students involved in activities, such as building a float, or doing an experiment. The content is familiar and can make ESL students feel more a part of the school while learning vocabulary.

Once students have mastered the basic vocabulary, go beyond the school into the community.

❑ **Use magazines.** Many how-to magazines, such as *Handyman*, show step-by-step procedures for building things. Pasted on wallboard and laminated, these can be used over and over.

❑ **Use cartoon strips.** Cut out frames of a cartoon strip. Blank out the words in the "bubbles" and have students fill them in with their own dialogue.

Use the Language Experience Approach (LEA)

The Language Experience Approach is one of the most effective reading strategies we have encountered. Simply stated, students dictate stories to the teacher who records them, using the students' own vocabulary, grammar, and life experiences to form the basic reading material.

The experience consists of several discrete steps. You can vary them according to time, size of groups, and purpose.

STEPS IN LEA

1. **Experience something together.** This can be a field trip, a special event such as Valentine's Day, a shared story, a poem, a book, an activity such as baking cookies, a movie, or even something as simple as examining and eating marshmallows.

2. **Discuss the event together.** This step is critical. Because the emphasis is on discussion as they describe or recall the event, students make gains not only in oral development, but as they analyze the event, in the intellectual growth needed for success in reading.

3. **Write the story on chart or butcher paper.** Have each student contribute a sentence (unless you are working with a very large group, in which case you can elicit sentences from different children over a successive number of LEA sessions).

   Write each sentence, saying aloud each word that you write. "Mary said, 'I saw a giraffe,'" or "Mohammed thinks that kids' behavior is the hardest thing to adjust to in this country."

   When you have written a number of sentences or completed the story, reread the sentences, moving your finger under each word as you read it to reinforce left to right progression. Answer any questions that might come up.

   Have the students read orally with you?

   Have individuals read the sentence they have dictated?

4. **Have the students copy their own sentences or the entire story on paper.** If you haven't elicited a sentence from each student, you can now go around the room and encourage each one to generate his own sentence on the topic.

5. **Follow up the activity.** The experience does not stop with the writing. Other related activities can be included over the next few days.

> Refresh the students' memory by rereading the story, then have individual students read it in its entirety.

> Cut the words apart and have the students put them in correct order.

> Reinforce skills and sight words by calling on individual students to, for example, "Show me a word that begins with *m*," or "Where does it say *giraffe*?"

> Ask "What words do you know?" Underline these words and have students place them in their word banks.

> Have each student illustrate his word or sentence, or even the entire story.

The Language Experience Approach has many features to recommend it:

THE BENEFITS OF LEA

- All the language skills are used at once—reading, writing, speaking, and listening.

- Words from the students' own vocabularies are used. Students have no trouble reading words like *hippopotamus* or *Lamborghini* when they come from their personal store of experiences.

- Skill building, such as sight-word vocabulary or letter identification, can be promoted within a meaningful context.

- Oral vocabulary is increased.

- Self-concept is enhanced. A student can look at a page or a book of collected stories with pride and say, "I wrote that."

- The approach is appropriate for all age levels, kindergarten through adult.

- Less proficient students can benefit from seeing text that more proficient students have generated about topics they understand.

- The students' points of view are valued.

- LEA can be done in the students' native language, which is especially useful when the students are illiterate.

□ The content is authentic. Because the approach uses the students' own language based on their own experiences, it is immediately relevant; therefore their interest and motivation will be high.

□ The approach can be used in large groups, small groups, or with individuals, either as chart stories with the entire class, or as dictated stories written individually onto sheets of paper.

DO'S AND DON'T'S WITH LEA

When using LEA with ESL students, there are several things to remember:

■ **Do *not* use LEA to teach new concepts.** Here you are building and reinforcing language already learned. The students' first stories might only be a few sentences, or even a few words long, such as *Hmong house*. That's fine; it is still reading and is meaningful to your students.

■ **Write exactly what students say.** Do *not* reproduce their accent. If someone says, *I lost my chooz*, when he means *shoes*, write *shoes*.

■ **Do *not* make corrections to grammar, word choice, or organization.** Zing and Ha, for instance, after several rousing enactments of *Caps for Sale* (in which Barb always had to play the monkey), wrote the following summary, partly reproduced below:

> *He wore them on his head. No one buy some hats. And he sat down on a tree, because no one buy her cap. Her leg were tired. He went to sleep. He wake up. He see no cap on her head. The monkeys had the hats. He looked up high and saw the monkey.*

While you are transcribing their story, it is very tempting to write in *the*, correct the pronoun to the masculine gender, and add the plural *s* to *cap* and *leg*. There are several important reasons not to make corrections:

□ The goal of LEA is to make print meaningful for the students so that they can acquire reading skills. If you have made changes, and students attempt to read back their work as they originally stated it, they might become confused. In the writing example above, the teacher actually changed *buy* to *bought*; the children could not read the word because they did not know it.

□ Your goal is to write a story that reflects the learners' thoughts and language, not to develop a perfectly stated essay. If you focus on surface errors rather than the meaning, you are not only missing the point of the lesson, you are giving the students the impression that correctness is the most important thing, and that you are more concerned with form than with content.

❑ To change students' thoughts is to reject the legitimacy of those thoughts. It isn't their writing anymore, it's *yours*. Accepting what they say in English during these sessions does much to bolster their self-confidence.

Many teachers feel that if we don't correct students we reinforce their errors. However, put in their proper perspective, errors can be considered as a reflection of a stage of language development— a transitional state that will eventually disappear. These errors are important for you as a teacher, because they give you a written record of what each student knows—and does *not* know—in English. The errors in the example, *buy, her, leg*, for instance, show you what Zing and Ha need to learn in the future.

Once it has been written, you can go back over the story and ask students if they want to make any changes. At that point they might very well see the errors they have made and change them themselves. If not, you can point out the errors and give them the correct form—a much more valuable learning experience than making changes yourself during the writing process, and one that does not disrupt the students' trains of thought while they are composing.

During the course of the school year you can return to these stories with the students to demonstrate just how much progress they have made in English.

■ **Be extremely sensitive when including ESL students in large-group language experience activities.** Many ESL students are shy, feel hesitant about speaking (particularly in a group situation), and generally hover on the fringe of activities. ESL can be a great confidence booster if what the students have to say is important both to you as their teacher and to their fellow classmates. If each is listened to attentively, the importance given to what they have to say can cause great gains in their self-image. Sadly, though, students often will laugh at newcomers for their poor pronunciation or sentence structure. More advanced students might say something like, "Don't call on Lagi, she doesn't know anything." Educate your students to understand that ESL does not equal STUPID, and allow the newcomers the time and the opportunity to contribute to the best of their abilities.

At more advanced levels, or in the content areas, use LEA as a tool to elicit thoughts and brainstorm ideas. You are not looking for perfection, merely ideas, and all students can participate.

Use Literature

The Language Arts Framework implemented in California, and similar programs in many other forward-looking states and provinces throughout North America, have mandated the use of literature in the classrooms at all levels instead of the traditional basal/workbook method used for decades. ESL students do not need to be excluded from literature studies, even though their proficiency and reading skills may be weak. Young children do not need to wade through basal readers before being introduced to literature. Older students need not be consigned to the high-interest low-vocabulary books from the reading lab. Good fiction is available for all ages. Young-adult fiction for middle- and high-schoolers can motivate poor readers and help bridge the gap between their current level of proficiency and the language competence they need for success in academic English. At the secondary level, a survey course with a set number of books including those such as *Great Expectations* and *Tess of the d'Urbervilles* is obviously not the appropriate choice, but at all levels, students can read and enjoy literature.

CHOOSING BOOKS

Choosing books need not to be a major problem. Books for low-proficiency readers don't have to be dull, bland, or condescending. As parents have begun to pay more attention to their children's reading, the book industry has responded, and there has been a virtual explosion of good books for children and young adults in the past few years. There is a wide array of fiction and non-fiction books available, appropriate for content areas as well as for reading pleasure. Most of these books are short with simple plots and language that is within the learner's grasp.

For starters, any book on the Newbery or Caldecott Award list, or Children's Book Centre books (in Canada) are excellent reading. Nancie Atwell, author of *In the Middle*, suggests authors like Robert Cormier, Lois Lowry, Madeleine L'Engle, and Robert Lipsyte. Browse through your favorite bookstore. Go to book fairs. Find out what kids are reading and enjoying.

AN APPROACH TO TEACHING LITERATURE

The following strategy is appropriate for all levels, primary through senior high school. It is an approach that focuses on enjoying literature as literature, rather than reading literature solely to learn reading skills. Reading becomes the end rather than a means to an end; readers become better readers as a consequence of loving to read. In this approach the teacher is a participant, a member of the readers' club rather than the source of knowledge and the inquisitor who asks questions to check up and test knowledge.

With this strategy there are two readings of each book. The first is simply for pleasure and comprehension, to find out what happened, get a feeling for character and setting. The readers respond as readers, both to the story and to the enjoyment it brings them. The second reading is analytical, to look at the text as writers, and to examine how the author crafted the book so that the readers found the plot exciting and the characters believable.

Two readings are important for ESL readers. The first time, they may struggle through the story with only partial understanding. This may be for a variety of reasons: their insufficient background knowledge, the difficulty of the reading level, and the fact that they are unaccustomed to the style of English language literature. On the second reading, the discussion and responses of other group members will help to increase understanding, and readers can go over now-familiar material with added comprehension and enjoyment.

It is not necessary to require ESL students to read entire books or understand everything. You are simply working toward competency and skill. No high school student will be able to understand a book as well as you if you have read it six times and studied it in three college courses. We cannot expect depth and perception from beginners; we *can* expect progress.

In approaching a piece of literature, whether a short story, novel, play, or simply a child's story, follow these steps:

STEPS TO BE TAKEN

1. **Choose several different books, and obtain about six copies of each.** Find books that are well written and that appeal to students in some way.

2. **Do a sales job on each one to get the students interested:** tell them what each is about; read them a few choice lines.

3. **Have each student then choose which one they want to read.** The selection is based upon their interest, not your judgment of what is appropriate. In this way, "reading groups" are determined by students' interest, not by the built-in reading levels of basal readers.

4. **Meet with each group and have them decide how long it will take them to read the book.**

5. **Get students to read independently.** Don't give them specific things to look for, simply tell them to write down anything they find particularly interesting or that they want to remember and talk about. Elementary students can be given pads of "stickies" (note pads with adhesive) with which to mark things they noticed in the text. Older readers can keep running

journals of what they notice. These may be response journal entries, guided by such questions as, "Who did you relate to in the story? Tell about one time in your life when you felt like this character did."

6. **When the group meets at the agreed-upon time, begin the conversation with "How was the book?"**

7. **As they talk, write notes on their discussion,** being careful to look down most of the time so that the students are forced to talk to each other, not to you. Contribute your thoughts and opinions and point out your favorite parts, but don't let the class discussion follow the traditional teacher-led format.

   This stage is the most important, not only for the ESL student, but for poor, or less-proficient readers. The discussion will clarify for students what they read, what they didn't understand, and the points they missed. They will be swept along by the discussion. They may not get much out of the book on the first reading, but, after the discussion, will read it for the second time with much more comprehension and enjoyment.

8. **Proceed to the second, or analytical reading,** using the students' comments you have written down, such as, "The fat lady was awful. I just wanted to strangle her."

9. **Have students then do the revised reading.** In this reading, students look for specific techniques the author used to make the reader respond.

10. **Have them look for specific writing techniques.** Ask questions such as, "You said you couldn't stand the fat lady. What did the author write to make you feel that way?" In this way, the students see themselves as writers, noticing how an author can reveal character through actions, dialogue, and so on.

11. **In this second reading group, have students discuss the details of the author's style.**

12. **As a follow-up, have students demonstrate their understanding non-visually** by mapping the relationships between the main characters, illustrating a book cover or a major scene, making puppets and putting on a puppet show, or writing a story of their own on a similar theme.

AN ALTERNATIVE APPROACH

If you have large numbers of poor or non-readers you may consider this alternative.

1. **Choose a story** such as *I Know an Old Lady*. Give one copy to each child in the group, or if that isn't possible one to every two children.

2. **Get the children thinking about the theme of the story.** Ask them if they have ever eaten too much, and how they felt when they did.

3. **Read the story aloud, with the children following in their books.** When they are familiar with the language pattern, you can have them finish parts of the text from memory.

4. **Read the story a second time, discussing difficult vocabulary words** as they appear in the text. Have the children guess the definitions based on context, prior knowledge, or cues from the illustrations.

5. **Have pairs of children read the story aloud,** with each partner having a chance to read.

6. **Discuss the sequence of the story.** It may be useful to make sentence strips to be placed in a pocket chart and arranged in the correct order.

7. **Have a follow-up to the story.** For instance, let the students write a continuation of the story in two or three sentences. For example, "What could she swallow to catch the horse?"

8. **Have the children illustrate their endings.**

Working With Different Levels of Readers

Most of all, students need someone to guide them in their acquisition of English and reading skills. Following are strategies you can use for different levels of readers.

WITH ILLITERATE STUDENTS

What do I do with those students who are illiterate in their own language?

With illiterate students you must start from scratch. They might not know things that are so basic to reading that we take them for granted:

> How to hold a book and turn pages
> That the markings on the page communicate meaning
> What a word is
> That in English, print moves from left to right

Unless students interact with print, they won't learn any of these things; therefore, you need to involve them in as many activities as possible that include print. The foundation for students' readiness to read and write is their understanding that the language they hear and speak can be represented in print.

As noted in chapter 4, we strongly advocate the whole language approach. Instead of teaching word-attack skills and sight vocabularies, comprehension should be the priority. However, we recognize that there are certain things that your preliterate students need to know. As Bell and Burnaby, in *A Handbook for ESL Literacy* (1984), point out, people who know that a cow is a cow whether it is facing left or right do not automatically recognize that the differences between *p, b, d* and *q* are significant. They need some training in pre-reading skills that involve shape recognition.

George Rathmell, in *Bench Marks in Reading* (1984), has listed the necessary pre-reading skills:

❑ Ability to recognize similarities and differences in shapes, letters, numbers, and words

❑ Ability to arrange items in a sequence, such as smallest to largest, beginning to end, left to right, including classifying items into categories and arranging pictures into a logical narrative order

❑ Ability to recognize letters and numbers

However, the teaching of pre-reading skills needs to be put in proper perspective and not be allowed to take priority or become focused upon to the exclusion of all else. A balanced program of interaction with real texts, supplemented by practice in visual discrimination, is essential.

Use real manipulables rather than dittoed exercises. For example, you can make a collection of articles such as

❑ Buttons, rocks, shells, leaves, flowers

❑ Stones, nuts, beans, marbles, metal objects

❑ Cloth, feathers, corks, bottle caps

❑ Ice cream sticks, straws, toothpicks, blocks

Possible activities include

❑ Sorting according to properties: size, color, shape, texture, flexibility, order, number of holes

❑ Math: weighing, measuring, graphing, adding, subtracting, counting, comparing, estimating, collecting, categorizing

❑ Language arts: describing, defining, sharing discoveries

These activities can be done individually or in small groups. Create a special corner in which a collection of various manipulables is always available.

Where should I start?

First encounters with reading must be interesting and of practical value. Help students learn the most useful vocabulary.

■ Start with their names. Children—and adults—derive intense satisfaction from seeing their own names in print, and will copy them many times, learning the names of the letter as a matter of course. A Chicano woman once came into Barb's ESL night class. She was an illiterate migrant worker who wanted to know how to write her name. Barb wrote *Maria* on a piece of paper, whereupon Maria spent the next forty-five minutes practicing. When she was satisfied she left. She never returned; she had learned the one thing she had come for.

■ Go on from the students' names to the survival words they have learned. They can then make word cards for their desks, chairs, and so on, advancing to other items in the room.

At the elementary level

■ Raid the preschool and kindergarten for shapes, colors, numbers, and so on. Begin with very simple exercises, such as recognizing triangles versus circles, then move on to more difficult tasks, such as matching letters or words.

■ Stock your room with wordless picture books. During free reading allow children to browse through these, or have a buddy or aide discuss the pictures.

At the secondary level, vocabulary should include

■ Names of teachers

■ Their own addresses, telephone numbers, and other words they need to know to fill out forms

■ Common signs (*Men, Women, Help, Exit*)

■ High frequency words (classroom objects, home objects, public transportation, names of businesses and public buildings, facilities in the community, and so on)

■ Basic subject-matter vocabulary, equipment, common instructions and procedures

■ Days, months, expression of time

What do I do when students don't know their alphabet?

Perhaps your students are preliterate. Or maybe they can read, but in languages that use a written system other than the Roman alphabet. They might read characters such as Chinese, or non-Roman alphabets such as Arabic, Hebrew, or Thai. What do you do to teach them our system?

Students need to know the alphabet, the words and shapes associated with each letter. The sequence, useful for dictionary work, can be learned much later when this skill has some purpose. At the very least, students must be able to look at the written forms of letters, be able to trace, complete, and copy letters. This raises another question of priorities.

Anyone who has already learned to read has the skills needed to understand print. Learning the alphabet before meaningful reading is pointless. Don't spend large amounts of time teaching the alphabet while holding off on other learning. Students can learn these within the context of meaningful vocabulary.

For all levels

- Begin with the suggestions for illiterate students
- Use the language experience approach (LEA)

At the elementary level

- Practice one letter a day. Give each of the children cards, for example, one with the letter *r* on it, and have them find all the words that begin with *r* in the room or on the chart-stories children have elicited.
- If you don't already have one, find a large chart of the alphabet to display prominently. You can also buy or make individual strips to tape to each child's desk for easy reference.
- Have "name banners" with the names of your students hung around the room for the ESL students to refer to when practicing letter writing and letter recognition.

At the secondary level

- Begin utilizing the suggestions noted for elementary children.
- Use high interest, low-level reading books.
- Use picture dictionaries.
- Find books that the students are familiar with in their own languages. If you can find stories translated from the students' languages, the familiar content will guide their comprehension in the new language. Find a copy of a story Bible, or perhaps the Koran, or fairy and folk tales from their countries.

Do I need to teach phonics?

THE ROLE OF PHONICS

There is a great deal of disagreement among experts concerning this issue. Some believe that reading cannot begin until the basic phonics rules have been mastered. On the other hand, some experts, such as Frank Smith, noted author of such classic reading texts as *Reading Without Nonsense* (1985), claim unequivocally that teaching phonics simply does not work, that the rules of phonics are so complex and unreliable as to be utterly confusing. Others go so far as to state that giving phonics lessons before the children have discovered the pleasure of stories is a sure way to set up failure. Which view is right?

Much as they need to know the alphabet, children need to know some basic sound–letter correspondences. They need to be familiar with the various sounds each letter can represent. Many of our words *do* follow consistent patterns, and these can be relied upon to build word-attack skills.

Teaching phonics exclusively, however, ignores meaning. When introducing phonics, use only *known* words, not isolated sounds. Reading, writes Sarah Gudschinsky, author of *A Manual for Preliterate Peoples* (1973), should not begin with anything smaller than a word. Sound–letter correspondences can be learned and reinforced within the context of "real" reading. The U.S. National Commission on Reading states that, "Phonics instruction should aim to teach only the most important and regular of letter-to-sound relationships, because this is the sort of instruction that will most directly lay bare the alphabetic principle." This means teaching consonants that have only one sound, such as *m*. The Commission goes on to state that, "Once the basic relationships have been taught, the best way to get children to refine and extend their knowledge of letter–sound correspondences is through *repeated opportunities to read*." [The italics are ours.]

Of course, in the primary grades children can learn basic sound–letter correspondences along with their classmates, but with older students, the more time spent learning these in isolation, the more time is taken away from reading itself—and constant drilling is tedious and boring. Before they realize that the skills they are learning will eventually lead to reading, the students may become discouraged. Insistence on mastery of phonics may lead to more and more discouragement. The time allotted for phonics drill should be minimal in relation to activities spent encountering meaningful print.

While it is true that sounding out words is an important word-attack skill, it is not necessarily true that a word will be meaningful once it has been sounded out. For example, an English speaker might be able to "read" a Spanish text so that a Spanish speaker could understand what he's saying. However, if the reader's Spanish is so limited he cannot understand more than the occasional word, he is only barking at print. The same principle applies to English words. Anyone with reasonable word-attack skills can sound out the word *calumniate*. However, knowing how it should be pronounced doesn't give one any clue as to what it means. The meaning must either come from the context of the sentence or from a dictionary.

Good readers read for meaning. Poor readers are so busy decoding words that they cannot concentrate on meaning, and often lose the thread before they reach the end. Second-language readers, even though they may be fluent readers in their first language, tend to resort to poor strategies, such as reading word-for-word, working out every word laboriously. Thus, too much stress on sounding out words limits readers' strategies for getting meaning, and also stresses correctness over understanding. Students must learn to focus on context and use syntax as a way of predicting meaning, rather than learning only to sound out words.

The problem of learning the sound–letter correspondences is particularly difficult for children whose first languages don't discriminate between sounds that are distinctive in English. We have all heard jokes about "flied lice" and "rotsa ruck." This is because Japanese and Chinese speakers hear one sound where English speakers hear two. Cree speakers don't have *sh* in their language and will say *sip* for *ship*. Arabic speakers do not distinguish between *p* and *b*. One Arabic student confided that writing was a "pig broplem" for him. Concentrating upon these individual sounds when the student cannot distinguish them is pointless. Even if Li can't say *rice* the way we might wish it or distinguish the *l* and *r* sounds, if he knows the difference between *lice* and *rice*, he will never make an error in the context of a story. Eventually he will be able to hear the difference, but until then you have better things to do than drills between minimal pairs.

There are many ways to embed phonics instruction within meaningful context:

- Work on sound–letter correspondences using words elicited in a language experience activity (LEA).

- Teach rhymes that focus on one particular sound.

- Pick out known words that begin with the same letter and have the students put them in their word dictionaries or on word cards with illustrations.

- Use your name banners to illustrate beginning and ending sounds.

- Use the student-made dictionaries to illustrate words that begin with certain sounds.

WORKING WITH STUDENTS WHO ARE LITERATE IN THEIR FIRST LANGUAGE

What if the language students have first learned to read moves from right to left, or bottom to top?

Although languages such as Arabic, Persian, and Hebrew use an alphabetic system, they are read from right to left; Japanese is read from bottom to top. The problem of switching ESL students to left-to-right reading is resolved primarily through modeling. Students who are already literate will have learned proper eye-movement; now it needs to be reinforced in the proper direction.

READING/WRITING IN THE CORRECT DIRECTION

Several methods can ensure that students move from left to right when they read or write:

- Monitor their initial reading experiences, making sure that they are reading correctly

- When reading aloud, move your finger under the words you are reading.

- Provide a guide for the first few reading and writing experiences, such as arrows on the top of the page, or traffic lights showing green on the left and red on the right.

My students are literate in their first language. Where do I go from here?

One only learns to read once, but reading in one's first language helps reading in the second. "Learning to read in the native language," writes Robert Miller in *The Reading Teacher* (1982), "is beneficial because the learner brings many reading behaviors to the learning of a second language: vowels, consonants, blends, diphthongs, and the concepts of words, phrases, sentences, and punctuation. As the student masters the primary language, more and more skills can be transferred to the second language."

DEVELOPING SECOND–LANGUAGE LITERACY

In the best of all possible worlds, ESL students would either learn to read or continue to receive reading instruction in their native languages. However, few schools provide competent bilingual teachers for this purpose, so you're on your own.

- Start with material the students already know. If you can find stories translated from their own language, such as *Momotaro* from the Japanese, the familiar content will guide the students' comprehension in the new language.

- If at all possible, allow students to continue reading in their own language. This will help them master the skills and fluency needed to be efficient readers in English.

- Encourage literate parents to read to the children in their own language; this is one of the best ways to support their child's intellectual development. Parents are often under the erroneous impression that they cannot help their child because they cannot speak or read in the new language.

- Augment use of translated materials (if available) with LEA—the language experience approach.

- Have aides, peers, or older students read to them as often as possible, identifying known words and discussing content.

- Allow time for reading assisted by tapes.

Aiding Comprehension in Both Language Arts and the Content Areas

What if the students have a reasonable sight-word vocabulary, but still cannot comprehend simple materials?

FILLING IN THE GAPS

ESL learners face many difficulties in reading a second language: vocabulary, differences in style between written and spoken language, poor study skills, and lack of background knowledge. The buzzwords *into*, *through*, and *beyond* are particularly important. We need to help them get *into* the text, make it *through* the reading with comprehension, and apply the skills they have learned *beyond*, to other reading tasks.

GETTING THEM *INTO* THE TEXT

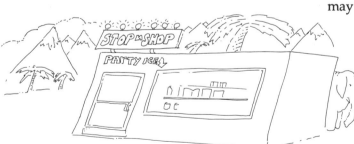

Reading depends on knowledge—not just about words and sound–letter correspondences, but also about the world. The reader brings the sum total of his personal experiences to reading. Refugee or migrant students, or those from remote reservations, may have either a very limited range of experience in terms of the school environment, or their life experiences may have been totally different from those in the stories they encounter. Those who have spent most of their lives in refugee camps will not have the background knowledge to understand what we might consider a simple story about shopping in the big city. We cannot take for granted that just because the vocabulary is limited the story will be easy to understand. There must be a contact point—some core of knowledge to begin with, or they will not understand.

For instance, Miguel was struggling to read a story about pancakes, making many errors, and obviously getting very little from the reading. His teacher asked him, "Miguel, do you know what pancakes are?"

With companions all around who had been remarking on how they loved pancakes, Miguel assured her that he did.

"Do you eat them very often?"

"Every day."

"What do you like on your pancakes?"

He rubbed his tummy. "Salt. Yummy."

Preparation for reading is a crucial part of the whole act of reading, whether at the elementary or secondary level, in language arts or in the content areas. It should not be slighted or skipped because it often determines whether that day's lesson will be a success or a failure for the student.

Emphasize the pre-reading segment of any reading task. The U.S. National Commission on Reading notes that although pre-reading is the most important part of any reading lesson, it is certainly the most neglected. Pre-reading involves more than simply deciding which words will be difficult and discussing them beforehand. The pre-reading process should include

❑ Discussing the content first

❑ Reading the selection aloud to your students before they read it themselves, helping them with difficult concepts and words

❑ Showing a related filmstrip or a movie

❑ Going on a field trip related to the subject

❑ Having students brainstorm and share what they know about a topic before introducing the text

❑ Predicting what will happen by looking at the pictures accompanying the text

MAKE IT *THROUGH* THE READING WITH COMPREHENSION

ESL readers often arrive at school with poor study skills. They do not know how to extract information from a text, or how to read for the purposes demanded. They need extensive practice with the varied tasks of reading in the content areas. Here again, the pre-reading segment of any reading task is critical. In addition to the suggestions above, we recommend that you

■ **Raid the remedial reading lab.** Often there are simple reading selections and books that target specific skills, but that are also interesting and at a level that is not condescending to the student.

■ **Ensure that students know what they are expected to get out of the reading selection**: the main idea, a general understanding, or specific facts to be recalled later.

■ **Ensure that students know what is required when answering any comprehension questions.** If presented with a choice, do they need to pick out which statements are true or must they put the sentences in order? Is there more than one correct answer?

■ **Walk the students through the reading selection, pointing out clues that aid comprehension,** such as pictures, maps, italics, boldface print, and so on.

■ **Help them look at print configurations,** such as the sizes and shapes of words, italics and boldface print, for clues to the relative importance of the information.

■ **Help them recognize what to look for.** Often readers get hung up feeling they need to know each word before they can go on to the next, thus spending an inordinate amount of time looking up words in the dictionary. Help them look for key words in a selection, such as the nouns and the verbs, then predict the meaning of the entire sentence based on these key words.

APPLY SKILLS LEARNED *BEYOND*, TO OTHER READING TASKS

ENCOURAGE EXTENSIVE READING

Encourage extensive reading at a similar or easier level than regular class members. Find selections that will help promote competency in the strategies students have learned.

■ Have a classroom discussion about students' outside reading.

■ Have students keep journals that record what they've read.

■ Allocate time to talk with each student individually about their current reading. Get to know their individual likes and dislikes so that you can steer them toward books that interest them.

■ Read other works by the same author, books of the same genre, or on the same topic.

■ Retell the story through another medium, such as film, drama, radio drama, or through another literary form such as poetry, drama, or song.

■ Write class (or school) newspapers, and/or magazines, relating to the topic.

- After they've completed reading something, have a discussion to see if students' attitudes, ideas, and interpretations have changed.

An Enabling Environment

Stephen and Susan Judy, authors of *The English Teacher's Handbook* (1983), write, "The fundamentals of literacy are mastered only in an environment that invites skill development rather than penalizing it. Too often schoolrooms inhibit the development of literacy by punishing kids for skill deficiencies, rather than concentrating positively on extending that range of skills students have already mastered."

We often get hung up on correcting mistakes, particularly in reading. Many times, teachers have students read aloud as a way of checking their comprehension. When students are reading along and stumble over a word, it seems intuitively right to jump in and correct them, but this must be done only with caution.

We want to state at the outset that we feel that asking individual students to read aloud is usually pointless. It is often needlessly stressful, and, more important, not a good indicator of how well or how much a reader is comprehending.

Some readers can read aloud perfectly—they sound wonderful, but comprehend little or nothing. Sixth-grader José, for instance, was turned over to tutors and classroom aides for two or three hours each day. The tutors were told that he needed practice in reading, and so he spent most of that time reading to them. He sounded good; he made few mistakes and seemed to read fluently. However, when asked what he had read, he couldn't tell them. The enormous amount of time and effort spent was not furthering his reading ability at all. This time could have been much better spent by reading to him, having him read silently from books he was familiar with, or using the language experience approach.

Other readers seem to stumble over every other word, making the task of listening to them particularly discomfiting. The temptation is to jump in and help. However, errors in reading aloud do not necessarily mean that the reader is not able to understand the text. Reading specialists Kenneth and Yetta Goodman prefer to call errors "miscues"—the difference between what the reader says orally and what is actually printed on the page. Some errors are "better" than others. If a student is reading aloud and reads "she went into her home" when the text says "she went into her house," no meaning is lost. If a student reads "the boy say a horse" when the text reads "the boy saw a house," this reader has lost the meaning of the sentence. Many students bumble and stumble their way through a text making error after error, but still retain the basic meaning and understand what the story is about. Comprehension is the main goal. Correcting students while they are reading distracts them from the main task of reading for meaning, places an emphasis of correctness and accuracy over comprehension, and may lead to passive, timid readers who will not proceed without help.

A better way of checking is simply to ask them, "What was the story about? Tell me what it said." "Did you understand this word? What does it mean?" "What happened after the villagers were unable to cut off the Chinese brother's head?" These types of questions lead the students back into the text, and you have a much clearer idea of how much they understood than if they simply read to you.

In most North American elementary classrooms, reading time is built around the round-robin reading group. We feel that reading aloud is helpful only when you have a specific reason for doing so, such as diagnosing students' reading strategies.

Eliminate the round-robin reading circle. A survey of elementary school children that asked them what turned them on or off reading, showed that children unanimously chose round-robin reading as the ultimate "turn-off." It can be a painfully embarrassing time for poor readers and for ESL students with noticeable accents. It is also boring for the others in the group as they sit waiting for their classmate to stumble through a passage. Do you remember, as a child, how often you just counted ahead to the sentence you knew you were going to be asked to read, rehearsing it while the others read, missing not only the story, but the point of the lesson? Time is spent more profitably when you ask children to read on their own, while you work on comprehension with individual students.

Conclusion

When we teach reading, these are our underlying assumptions:

- Reading must be for meaning.

- We learn to read by reading.

Reading does not happen in a vacuum. Readers need repeated opportunities to practice. They need someone to help them over the rough spots and teach them strategies to get *into*, *through*, and *beyond* a text. And they need a comfortable environment in which they can attempt to read without fear of being jumped on for their mistakes. By providing these, we can move our learners from confused non-readers, to competent readers able to tackle any reading text or task.

WRITING

In this chapter, we will look at acquiring the skill of writing. We will focus on

- Using a process approach to writing with ESL students
- Helping students become better writers
- Commenting on student papers and assisting with revision
- How and when to correct errors

The Process Approach to Writing

Yesterday last night of the teacher Mary Eckes gaven would one to student all student in class—person doesn't get to have to know. This when student dd to get befor big one the squash all way came back to school at reach home family and nighbor. that right your are want to see becouse youre are doesn't have. doesn't know.

In the not-so-distant past, the emphasis in teaching writing was the "product." Students were given an assignment, which they completed and turned in. Their only audience was the teacher, who was judge, jury, and executioner. In such classrooms, a piece like the one above, written by Cham, would have come back bloodied with ink marks, graphically demonstrating what she didn't know. She would not have been given any chance to change her ideas or fix what was wrong, as the class would have gone on to another assignment. In the traditional classroom, this composition would undoubtedly have received a failing grade.

But research has revealed that writing is not a linear process in which writers start at the beginning and work through, error free, to the end. It is a cyclical process, in which the writer continually circles back, reviewing and revising. Some start with outlines, others just start, discovering as they go where they're headed. Most writers plan, compose, then read what they've written, edit as they go, write some more, revise a little, and so on.

Recognition of this process has influenced the teaching of writing; the emphasis has switched from *the product* to *the process* of writing. Real learning takes place during the process of putting thoughts down on paper. Writers, whether children or adults, do not become writers by simulating writing—by filling in blanks on dittoed sheets, by learning grammar rules, memorizing vocabulary, or practicing lists of spelling words. They learn to write by writing. "Real" writing—writing done for real purposes with real audiences—gives students a chance to practice penmanship, grammar, organization, and style, all within a framework of communication. Real writing is more than words or even sentences; it is "whole text" writing that involves "whole text planning," whether for a story, a letter, a journal, or an essay.

With ESL learners, one is tempted to focus first on vocabulary development, spelling, and grammar. However, this bottom-up approach returns to the use of such strategies as word drills that have limited instructional value. It also neglects the main goal of writing: to create meaning.

THE STAGES OF WRITING

Allow students time to work through all the stages of the writing process. Although these stages are not always discrete, or distinguishable from one another, the writing process can be divided into the following major steps:

1. **Pre-writing.** This is the thinking stage, perhaps the most important step for ESL students. It is a time for students not only to generate ideas, but to pool their collective knowledge of vocabulary and grammatical structure appropriate to the lesson. All students, ESL students in particular, need to have a great deal of stimuli before they write. The ESL student faces two major problems: 1) deciding what to say, and 2) how to say it. As a lead-in to writing, provide as much opportunity as possible for students to listen to and participate in discussions relating to the topics they will be writing about. Make pre-writing an important part of every writing activity.

   ❑ Read them stories. This is effective for kindergarten through high school. Reading aloud provides students with models for story writing by giving them a sense of story form, characterization, plot, drama, and so on. It also sparks their imagination, giving them ideas to write about.

- Brainstorm as a class, generating lists of ideas and possible topics.
- Take field trips.
- Listen to speeches.
- Show films, videos, or filmstrips.
- Read poems.
- Allow students to read and comment on each other's work.

2. **Organizing.** This is the stage in which students pull their thoughts together and make the initial decisions about where to start, points of view, characters, as well as the information they want to include.

3. **Drafting.** In this step, students actually put their thoughts on paper. This tentative exploratory stage can often be the hardest part; articulating what one is thinking can be a long and sometimes arduous process.

4. **Evaluating.** This can be a time for the students to read and judge their own work, and/or for others, either you or the students' peers, to read it. One-to-one or small-group sharing is important for feedback on meaning.

5. **Revising.** This is when changes should be made that affect meaning. Many beginning writers believe that once they have put their thoughts down on paper, they have reached the end; they are finished, and aside from correcting a few spelling errors they have nothing more to do. Students need to learn that authors often write passages many times before they are satisfied. Intervention by the teacher at this stage is critical. Guide your students by making suggestions for changes, by asking for clarification, and so on. Later in this chapter, we provide writing examples and discuss ways to help students revise their work.

6. **Editing.** Putting the final touches on a piece, polishing grammar, punctuation, spelling, and other mechanics should be done at this stage.

Helping Students Become Successful Writers

In order to learn to write well, every beginning writer needs

- To be immersed in writing
- An enabling environment
- Feedback and guidance from interested readers

IMMERSE STUDENTS IN WRITING

Being immersed in writing means not only frequent opportunities to write, but frequent opportunities to read not only finished products, but the ongoing work of other writers. To immerse your learners in writing

- **Make writing an everyday activity.** In order for learners to advance their writing skills, they must have constant opportunity to practice. Setting a block of time each day or several class periods per week for reading, revising, and seeking feedback is critical to learning advancement.

- **Make writing "real."** The writing must be for real purposes, with real audiences.

  - Write letters to the principal, to real authors, to heroes.

  - Produce newsletters or even full-fledged newspapers about class or school activities.

  - Prepare invitations to Parent's Night and school concerts.

  - Maintain two-way journals with other students.

  - Keep records of events, such as field trips, pet care, growth charts for plants, daily schedules, and so on.

- **Make writing meaningful.** In other words, find topics your students can "sink their teeth into," frequently allowing them to choose their own topics. All students write best about things they care about. Everybody knows how boring the "My Summer Vacation" assignments are, and how little one has to say. But students who are captivated by the need to say something about a topic that interests them will be carried along by their enthusiasm. A teacher trainee, who was tutoring three Chicano boys, struggled along at a basic level, until she discovered they were interested in wrestling. Their hero was Hulk Hogan. Together they wrote letters to Hulk. Their excitement carried them through the difficulty of articulating (in English) what they wanted to say, and the end result was much superior to anything they had produced before. At both the elementary and secondary levels, teachers have collected "Stories We Brought With Us"—tales from the homeland. These folk tales, fairy stories, legends, and myths had special meaning to the students who wrote them, and gave their fellow students a greater understanding of the rich cultural heritage the newcomers had brought to their adopted country.

- **Allow students to explore all forms of writing,** from poetry, to persuasive essays, to advertisements. Audience, topic, and purpose change with every new composition, as do form and style.

new world my father like to go to the new world because you ca. do everything like the way that know. we can go at the jungle, and cuting the wood to make a house, hunting, kithng, growing cros of. other thing that you wanted to do best for your life or family. than you can do every thing that you want by your own.

Academic writing differs from writing in personal journals, as letters differ from complaints about problems in the school. Students need practice in all areas.

■ **Provide time for both intensive and extensive writing.** *Intensive writing* is structured and written for a specific purpose. This is writing to be revised, writing where the specific skills of organization, mechanics, and editing can be taught. *Extensive writing* is not to be revised or corrected, it is used to articulate thoughts, explore new ideas, and gain fluency without the need to stop and worry about correctness. Journals, diaries, and learning logs are all examples of extensive writing.

PROVIDE AN ENABLING ENVIRONMENT

You need to be concerned not only with the fact of writing, but the setting in which students write and the response to their writing.

■ **Create a comfortable atmosphere.** Set up a climate of trust in which students believe that writing is important and that their writing is valued. Encourage them to take risks as writers, to experiment with different forms and styles without fear that their mistakes will be punished. Give them authority over their writing by allowing each of them to choose the topic and the style. Encourage students to exchange ideas and share drafts, to get feedback and ideas from each other. Above all, help them to understand that writing is a meaning-making event.

- **Make writing a collaborative act.** There is a myth that writing is a lonely act, done in solitude; this isn't necessarily true. Language is a social act and writing can be too. In observing writers truly engaged in writing, researchers have noted how they talk while they write, sharing their thoughts and their writing with other writers to get more ideas. Bilingual and non-native-English speakers often talk and write more when allowed to interact with their peers. Encourage this interaction.

  □ Promote collective writing of stories or plays.

  □ Provide time for sharing writing and ideas.

  □ Encourage and train peer editors.

- **Celebrate their writing.** When students write, they need an appreciative audience to read their writing and to offer them encouragement. The feedback students receive in response to their writing has a significant impact on how they perceive the writing process and how much they improve. Edelsky, in *Writing in a Bilingual Program: Habia Una Vez* (1986), noted that writing assignments that emphasize quantity alone, with no honoring of the writing by publishing or discussion, could even be destructive because they promote the idea that quantity is more important than quality. We suggest you employ some of the following strategies:

  □ Display students' writing on the wall for everybody to read.

  □ Have an "author's chair" as the seat of honor.

  □ Have an "Author of the Week" in which one student's writing is celebrated, pinned on a special area of the wall. Have other students interview the author about his writing.

  □ Publish the writing in the form of books, with hard covers the students make themselves.

  □ Create a special library of books written by the class.

  □ Provide a time for public reading of students' writing. At both elementary and secondary levels, students need to have the opportunity to be recognized and applauded for their efforts.

  □ Provide mailboxes for the students to write letters to you, or to each other.

  □ Produce "Readers' Theaters," using excerpts from students' writing.

- **Allow the students to write in their own language.** If they speak and write in a language you don't know, then of course you cannot read it. However, as with reading, writing in one language improves writing in another. Encourage them to write in English, but allow them to start in their own language, making the transition to English as they grow more confident in their abilities. Researchers such as Edelsky have noted that there is often no clear break from the ESL students' native language to English. Often these students will write in both languages within the same piece of writing for a while, until they feel safe or confident enough to write totally in English. Even fluent English speakers will substitute words in their own language during first drafts.

- **Model the writing process.** Watching a teacher working on a draft of a letter or essay can demonstrate that writing isn't a tedious boring task or a meaningless activity, but a satisfying creative act. Beginning writers need to see that writing is more than just dittoes and work sheets, a chore to get through; it is a wonderful way to articulate thoughts, one that can be enjoyable and exciting. Write while they are writing. Nancie Atwell, author of *In the Middle* (1987), advocates a "No Man's Land." When she is writing seriously, she is not to be interrupted.

  - Share your own drafts, asking students to comment and critique them.

  - Voice your own struggles to articulate your thoughts. Allow the students to see how a real writer goes from draft to draft in the search for precision.

- **Be patient.** Writing ability takes a long time to develop. ESL students come with different levels of competence; some are capable writers in their own language, others are barely literate. In a second language, they are asked to master a task with which many native-English speakers never become fully comfortable or proficient. With constant practice and the freedom to experiment and make errors, they will gradually achieve proficiency.

ENSURE GUIDANCE AND FEEDBACK FROM INTERESTED READERS

Beginning writers in both first and second languages need help with the writing process. They need guidance in making some of the larger decisions of writing, related to such things as topic, style, and form. They need feedback on how effectively they are communicating, direction as to how to improve, and help with specific points such as mechanics, spelling, and punctuation. Your role in implementing the enabling environment and helping writers grow is critical. But with ESL writers you must deal with a wide range of situations that you would not normally encounter if you had only native-English speakers. Following are some questions you may have concerning your students and their writing.

My students are illiterate. They don't even know their alphabet much less how to write a whole text. What do I do to help them?

WORKING WITH BEGINNERS

Write for them. Many students have never held a pencil before. The fine motor skills required for writing demand much effort on the part of beginning writers. Often just the act of trying to put letters on paper is so taxing it frustrates their efforts to express coherent thoughts. The temptation is to have them practice their ABCs until they have learned them correctly; however, these skills should be practiced only within the context of real writing. Practicing meaningful phrases, rather than words in isolation, reinforces meaning as well as skills. Don't wait until students can form sentences before allowing them to write. Even though they can't write, students have plenty to say; everyone has a story to tell. Encourage them to jump right in.

Researchers studying first-language learners have noted that children pass through a sequence of broad stages: scribbles; only a few letters, words, and illegible squiggles; a sentence or a series of several unrelated sentences; two or more related sentences. While we cannot apply these stages on a wholesale basis to non-English-speaking students, we can be aware of them and allow our students the freedom to experiment and learn, without imposing the need for perfection and precision immediately.

In chapter 5, "Reading," we discussed the language experience approach (LEA), in which the teacher writes the students' thoughts first, then has them copy what you have elicited. The word *fireman* might be a whole text for one student; accept it as such. After you have written their thoughts down for the students, they can copy your writing onto their own paper. They will make the transition to writing on their own when they are ready—when they have gained enough confidence to try, learned some vocabulary, or just simply learned that writing has meaning.

First-grader Rebecca, for example, did not seem to understand the basic speech-print connection. After many months of watching LEA in action, she began to copy the words the teacher provided on the board as springboards to thought. One day her teacher wrote the words *playground*, *soccer*, and *hopscotch* on the board. This is what Rebecca wrote:

> Our Playground.
> I Love hopscotch BKasakids.
> I loVe soccer Kids.

Translated, this meant, "I love hopscotch because of the kids. I love soccer because of the kids." For a first try at a real story, her piece is impressive. She shows that she understands the functions of print, and that she is aware of syntax, sentence structure and boundaries, as well as punctuation. She is also making a personal and lively statement about the topic. She loves soccer and hopscotch because of the kids who play the games with her. There is much to be praised and encouraged.

My students have good thoughts, but aren't organized at all. What can I do?

Provide scaffolds (models for writing) wherever possible. A scaffold is a framework on which students can hang their ideas. Scaffolds allow students to concentrate on content. Since scaffolds provide the forms, they help students learn how to organize at many levels: the grammatical level, the sentence level, the paragraph level, and the text level. Students model the scaffold, imitate it, and gain control over their writing.

There are many different types of scaffolds:

▫ Patterned poetry, such as haiku, cinquain, diamante, sonnets.

▫ Frame sentences. For example, in one elementary school classroom, after a unit on occupations, students made little books about themselves, each in occupational roles they thought they might enjoy. They wrote sentences according to the framework worked out together on the blackboard: "I am a _____ I wear a _____ uniform. Here is where I work. This is me working." They illustrated their books with pictures of themselves in their various roles.

Models are especially important in the upper grades and for the content areas as writers need to have examples of good writing in order to write well themselves. Find good examples—textbooks are one source—for them to use as guides. Provide them with positive models such as sample research reports or science results. With some instruction on how the sample is organized, students can follow the same format for clearer, more readable papers.

Some writing-process advocates feel that teaching structure such as the rhetorical modes (narrative, descriptive, argumentative, comparison and contrast, and so on) removes students' control over their written work. However, we believe that for ESL students, it is important to focus directly on organization. Most students born in North America have been exposed to writing from early childhood. After many years of reading stories, magazine articles, newspapers, and so on, they have internalized the organizational patterns that are common to each type of writing. So, when we ask them to write a story or compare two objects, for instance, they can do it with little difficulty. Many ESL students have not had the benefit of these years of reading and writing. While we can hope that our students will learn these patterns incidentally, without explicit instruction, during their exposure to writing, we cannot leave this to chance. In addition, many cultures and non-Western societies have different ways of organizing essays and stories. Students from these backgrounds need to be shown directly that, while their patterns are not actually incorrect, the structure can be confusing to English-speaking readers searching for a familiar pattern of organization. Form should not be imposed arbitrarily without regard for purpose or audience (i.e., "Today we're going to write a comparison/contrast paper"), but neither should we leave organization to chance.

Giving Constructive Feedback

My students make a lot of grammatical errors. What should I do?

CORRECTING ERRORS

The answer depends on the levels of the students and the purpose of the assignment. With younger children and newcomers, it is, at first, probably best to accept any effort on their part. If the language is totally garbled, the essays unstructured, and the main ideas obscure, don't correct the grammar. Instead, talk to the students about their ideas to help clarify what they really want to say.

> *Yesterday last night of the teacher Mary Eckes gaven would one to student all student in class—person doesn't get to have to know. This when student dd to get befor big one the squash all way came back to school at reach home family and nighbor. that right your are want to see becouse youre are doesn't have. doesn't know.*

Using the example above, find out what Cham is trying to say and how she wants to say it. In this case Cham was telling a story about a squash. Mary used to bring in produce from her garden and hold a lottery to determine which student would get the vegetables; no one knew who was going to win. Cham won on that occasion, and the prize was such a large squash that she shared half of it with her neighbor. With a little prompting, the story became clear and Mary could help her focus and clarify. Pointing out her grammatical errors at this point would have been harmful because she would have been discouraged.

This does not mean that errors should be completely ignored. We cannot focus solely on the process at the expense of the product. We must show a clear concern for mechanics. Quality and correctness *are* important issues because ultimately, we are writing to be read—and understood! Here again, it is a matter of priorities. As with reading, accuracy and skills should be secondary to meaning. We've all read the story or essay that is perfect mechanically and yet says nothing, while we've read others that are riddled with errors, and yet are spritely and creative.

Stress content more than correctness. Initially, getting the ideas out is the important thing; then they must be shaped until the writer achieves what he wants to say. Students need the chance to rewrite, as nobody writes the first draft perfectly. If students are worried about perfection, they will be afraid to be creative and experimental, sticking only to what they are sure of. Ammon (1985) noted that writers who feel they need to invest much of their time and energy to spelling and other component skills tire more quickly and eventually give up before they have finished. If your students are con-

> My Name is: Omar Al-Said
> My sister: Layla Al-Said
> My brother: Abdul Al-Said
> My Cousen: Khalid Joad
>
> I from Jordan My city name Agaba.
> my old are: seventeen and I born in 7/7/72
> I am living in Yahi City and I have three brother, one sister
> I live with my family and I have uncles in Los Angles
> I studying in Yahi City high school ang my grade is 11th
> I have priod Math and history, computer, PE and ESL and very priod easy for me because a teacher very much with me
> Y.C. is a very beautiful there is a tress and river and school and These are good and the weather is useful for our breathing
> When I lefted Jordan I come to los Angles by plane from seven month and and I moved do Yahi City after one and half month because the weather here better than los Angles.

cerned both with mechanics *and* getting their ideas out, they may be forced into a trade-off between attention to the one to the detriment of the other. In other words, as Frank Smith writes in *Reading Without Nonsense* (1985), "Emphasis on the elimination of mistakes results in the elimination of writing." Allow students plenty of time to make tentative efforts and sort out their ideas before asking them to wrestle with the problems of getting their writing to look and sound like native English.

Errors are not random but are strategies students employ when they have not yet learned or mastered a new form or concept. They show courage in trying something new. Celebrate mistakes; applaud students for daring something difficult. Errors can demonstrate both what the students know and what they have not yet learned. As with reading, we can view errors as valuable insights into the students' development and use them to pinpoint areas they need to work on. For example, if Wei Xia writes, "I am a youngest student in the class," it is clear that he needs to learn more about articles.

Publishing students' work in the form of newsletters and so on, will motivate them to correct and revise. If they have a stake in what is written, if their names are noted as authors and their work is out there for the world to see, they will be more concerned with perfection.

What should I correct?

Limit yourself to correcting one type of mistake only and ignore the rest for the time being. Marking every error students have made can be defeating; they won't know where to start, and will get so bogged down trying to correct all their errors that they may give up, and any momentum gained will have been lost.

Ravi Shorey lists a hierarchy of error categories:

1. The most serious errors are verb forms (agreement, tenses, and so on).
2. Next in importance are word-choice errors.
3. Less serious errors are articles and prepositions.
4. Spelling errors are the least serious of all.

We shouldn't expect total perfection, nor should we expect that if we correct a type of error once, it will never reappear. Unfortunately it isn't that simple. Mastering English is a long, often slow process. The English article system, for instance, which we native-English speakers take for granted, is a second-language learner's nightmare. What seems to work in one sentence is totally inappropriate in another. Often prepositions make no logical sense at all, so they must simply be memorized. For example, we speak of *in the street* as well as *in the box*, and *on the table* as well as *on time*. Before they can master English forms, non-native speakers need a great deal of exposure to the range of structures and meanings possible.

When allowing time for revision, remember the law of diminishing returns. When we are striving for fluency, working for perfection on each paper fosters frustration. Many times it is appropriate to allow the student one or two rewrites, then go on to something else. It is also appropriate to give them many opportunities to write for fluency alone, without correction, such as in journal-writing.

At what stage should I make corrections?

Instruction and correction in mechanics is most effective at the editing stage, in response to a particular need. For ESL students, error correction too early in the process (for example, during the first revision) is liable to curtail their creativity, because they feel forced to concentrate on being "right." Gadda, Peitzman, and Walsh, in *Teaching Analytical Writing* (1988), point out that correcting the mechanical points of a paper is like fine-tuning an engine, something you do only after you have replaced and repaired the major parts. Why should someone work hard to fix something when it may be completely overhauled or even scrapped altogether? If they correct the language first, they will be unwilling to change the content. Only after the paper is clear, well-organized, and thorough, should the student work on the fine-tuning of grammar, spelling, and so on.

The most logical way to make corrections is to allow two revision stages, one for content, the other for mechanics. Thus, **the writing process for ESL students would look like this:**

1. **Students compose.**

2. **Teacher or peers respond.** This first response is for content alone. Ideas, organization, and clarity are the priorities here. You can train your students to work as peer editors for this stage, to respond to the impact of the work, ask for more ideas, clarification, and expansion.

3. **Students revise to clarify, add detail, and reorganize.**

4. **Teacher or peers respond.** This response is for mechanics. What has not been cleared up through a second reading and self-editing can be worked on here, on a topic (such as articles or verb tenses) agreed upon by you and the student.

5. Teacher teaches grammatical points as necessary.

6. Students edit for mechanics.

With this sequence, students know when you will be focusing on the form of their papers, and won't be wasting their creative energy trying to remember the rules of grammar at that stage (although they can ask for and receive help in grammar at any point of their writing).

Third grader Claudio, age eight, wrote the following story:

My bug jumps higher than Superman. He runs faster than a airplane. He walks nice. His name is donkey. His hair is strawberries. He is super. That's all

RESPONDING TO STUDENTS' WRITTEN WORK

Claudio has made a terrific start. His comparison to Superman is very vivid. He needs specific guidance as to how and where to improve. For the first revision you might ask him to describe, in one or two more sentences, more detailed physical characteristics of his bug. You might ask him how big the bug is, how many legs he has, what color his body is, and so on. Until Claudio is comfortable with the process approach to writing, you probably should not make him rewrite the entire story at this point; instead, ask him to compose the details at the bottom of his paper, to be added to the body of the draft when he has finished getting all his ideas out. Tell him to capitalize *Donkey*, since it is a name. For elementary school children and beginning ESL writers, it is not appropriate to tell them that they have made an error and force them to figure out where and how to correct it on their own. In most cases, give a mini-grammar lesson and let it go at that. For instance, tell him simply that he'll rarely go wrong putting *an* before words that start with *a*, *e*, *i*, *o*, or *u*.

For his final draft, Claudio could recopy his story on a large sheet of paper, insert his new sentences in the right spot, and illustrate the story with a drawing of his bug.

Abdullah, wrote the following paper in response to the question, "Which English language skill is the hardest one for you?"

Which english language skill has been the hartest on. English is funy longuage that we sey some the and read o the such as secret, sure or surprise. That meen riting is the hardest one for me so I thik that I'm still week in spilling and I need riting coure, also I don't knew much vocapulary that hard for me, spilling or riting needs memorise to learn but my memory is not good so it is hard to rite will wheth out rong in spilling or problems. If I tell about the easiest one, I sey listening is more easy for me I have good improvment in it so not prob in it also me gramar is good one easy enough for me to learn but the pig broplem is vocapulary and spilling onthing is easy I can speek will and understand will with proctes every thing become easy sometimes I rite pregraph to improve my riting but still need it might be next term it becom brety good any how I don't like this laguage

An understandable first reaction upon seeing such a paper is shock, followed by a feeling of helplessness, if not despair. How does one respond when the problems are of such magnitude, when the spelling is clearly out of hand, the punctuation practically non-existent, and the meaning, in many places, is obscure? How does one untangle the various problems without overwhelming Abdullah and destroying whatever self-confidence he has?

Many of his errors may be performance errors—errors made because he was inattentive, careless, or preoccupied with getting the meaning out. For instance, Abdullah writes *language* once, then *longuage* and further on *laguage; hartest on* then *hardest one*. Upon rereading, he will probably correct these errors. One strategy you might employ is to have each of your students read their papers aloud to a peer or have the peer read it back. Many times they will correct themselves because what they write does not jibe with what they hear. Abdullah may hear where the sentences should begin and end, and put periods in their appropriate places. If he doesn't, you have an indication of where the gaps are in his knowledge. Those errors are the competence errors—made because he has not learned a particular grammatical point, word meaning, spelling, or rhetorical form.

Once he has had a chance to rethink his paper, it is your turn. Your response is critical and should be on content alone. Ideas, organization, and clarity are priorities. There is a logical order of thinking, which leads to clear statements. In answer to the question, "Which skill has been the hardest one?" he answers that writing is, and gives a graphic example of why: we say things one way, and then we write them another. (There is an *s* sound in *secret* and *sh* sound in *sure* and a *z* sound in *surprise*, and yet we write them all with *s*.) He states that he has trouble with spelling and vocabulary, an accurate assessment of his problems. Through his examples, one can sense his frustration at learning this difficult language. There are two important ways to respond to his paper, and you should employ them both:

1. As a reader. It is important for Abdullah to see how his paper has an impact on you personally. You can make inter-lineal-comments, such as "I have trouble with spelling too!" and "Good examples!"

2. As a teacher. On a separate sheet of paper make specific suggestions as to how to improve.

Peitzman and Seideler, in *Teaching Analytical Writing* (1988), give guidelines for commenting on students' papers:

❏ **Skim the entire paper before writing comments.** You may make comments, only to find the students answered your criticisms further on in the papers.

❏ **Address students by their names.** With each communication, you are responding to a real person, and starting out this way establishes a connection between the two of you.

❏ **With each student, begin by stating a major strength of the student's written work,** then pinpoint the nature of major weaknesses. Don't negate your praise with a *but* or *however*. Praise without reservation.

❏ **Be supportive in tone.** These essays are true accomplishments for those who are struggling to articulate their thoughts in a new language. Don't dampen their enthusiasm. The students are likely to try harder for someone who they know understands and is in their corner.

❏ **List text-specific questions and suggestions for change.** Note the places that worked particularly well. Notes at the bottom of their papers like "tighten" or "reorganize" will not help them. If the students knew how, they would have done so.

❏ **Phrase your comments tentatively when appropriate.** Students need to understand that there are often many ways to solve problems. On occasion you may mistake the intent of a student, and if you make rigid pronouncements about changes required, you could be destroying the entire paper and its worth. And, most important, remember that these are the students' papers, and they need to maintain authority over their own writing. They need to have the right to change as they see necessary to make their papers fit their plans.

❏ **Don't solve their problems for them.** Direct them, find the problems, but let the students work at solving them.

❏ **Close with encouraging remarks.** Show that you have confidence in their ability. For example: "Abdullah, your examples of the problems we have with spelling are very vivid. English is a funny language that frustrates many English speakers too. Your paper would be more readable if you reorganized. Your thoughts jump from spelling to writing to vocabulary to listening and back to spelling again. Why don't you look for your weaknesses in spelling and writing first, and try to figure out why you have those problems. Then move on to what you are good at. End on a positive note! You are very accurate when you look at your own problems, and your examples demonstrate just how difficult English can be."

❑   **Give them a chance to revise again.** On this draft you can edit for grammar and mechanics. This does not mean doing the work for him. Show Abdullah what is wrong, why, and then direct him in the most productive way to give him a better understanding of English usage. Don't correct every error he has made. (With a paper like this, you would wind up marking nearly every word, and Abdullah would be so defeated he might give up altogether.) Choose one. If he has not corrected his sentence boundaries by inserting periods and starting the next sentences with uppercase letters, that might be a good place to start.

Many students want—in fact insist—on having every error corrected. If this is the case, it is often fruitless to mark the spelling errors and tell them to look up the words. If they don't know how to spell the words in the first place, looking them up won't help. How can you tell Abdullah to look up *with* when he has spelled it *wheth*? Telling students how to spell words is not cheating, nor is it encouraging them to be lazy. You can incorporate the worst errors into each student's personal spelling plan discussed below.

Their spelling is terrible! If it is a low priority, should I ignore it altogether?

Poor spelling is one of the most noticeable errors that writers make, and it is also one that we are most inclined to condemn. Thus, many teachers feel that teaching spelling is important and that perfection is critical. Many educators also feel that allowing children to spell spontaneously and incorrectly will lead to bad spelling habits down the road. Experts, however, emphatically disagree. The McCrackens, for example, state that, "If conventional spelling is required initially, the [writing] program will fail, because the children will be inhibited from expressing their ideas in writing. They will fail to learn the alphabetic principle of written English, because conventional spelling obscures the sound–letter relationships."

SPELLING

Errors in spelling are not random. They are based on a student's stage of understanding of sound–letter correspondences. As with any other skill, children begin with gross approximations, gradually improving their accuracy. For example, when Rania draws a silly picture of Atosa and labels it *I am cucu*, or when Enrique writes *chack* for *chalk*, or Sabina writes *wich broom* under a drawing of a witch, they are demonstrating that they know a great deal, if not the finer points, of English spelling.

The McCrackens advocate making a chart of "doozers," words that are very common and yet resist phonetics, such as *once, the, of*. Keep this list displayed on the wall for easy reference.

Some schools use the "guess and go" approach, in which the child writes an approximation of what he wants to say, and comes back later with the correct spelling. This was what Rebecca (page 121) used. *Bksakids* was a very good try at *because of the kids*, and she wasn't hampered by the necessity to get it perfect the first time.

Errors tell you what students know, what they do not know, and what learning experiences they need. By noting which kinds of mistakes students make, you can set up individual spelling programs. Ronald Cramer, in *Writing, Reading and Language Growth* (1978), asserts that the key to a good spelling program is a good writing program. Rather than trudging through commercial spelling materials, he advocates setting up personal spelling programs for each student, developed from misspelling within the students' writings, from the functional word needs of each student, and from the additional words that the children have chosen for themselves. He cautions, however, that we not begin formal spelling instruction until the children have achieved at least a first-grade reading level.

Before this time, students should be allowed to progress on their own, with as much help as they need or desire from you. In most cases, it is best to simply supply the correct spelling of the word and let them continue.

USING COMPUTERS

Computers with word-processing functions can be very helpful to beginning writers. For some ESL students, it's easier to practice writing on a word processor than on paper. The word processor prints the letters of the alphabet perfectly, in neat straight lines. Their compositions, no matter how short, can be printed in a professional manner.

All steps of the creative writing process can be learned and practiced on a computer by individuals or groups. For example, a small group of both ESL and native-English speakers can work cooperatively on one computer. After brainstorming for pre-writing ideas, they can write their story without fear of making mistakes, not only because errors are seen as part of the writing process, but also because their errors will be so easy to correct. Revising and editing, when it is possible to delete and/or rearrange words, sentences, and paragraphs simply by pressing keys, is simple, and most students find it satisfying and fun. Writing second and third drafts of a paper is no longer tedious. Students are usually proud of their professionally printed final product and eager to start the next one.

```
A Groundhog was in a hole
It came out
And he saw his shadow
And he went back in
For a nice little nap
And slept
For six more weeks.
```

USING PEER TUTORS

Peer tutors can be a valuable asset in a writing classroom because they provide real audiences for students' work. But peer responses can often fall flat or fail altogether because students don't know what to say: they can't get beyond "I liked it," or can find nothing but fault. Train your students to know what to look for and how to give specific suggestions. Have them look at the content, not the grammar, finding parts they liked and parts that confused them or could have been written in more detail. It may help to give them a worksheet with specific tasks for them to complete, such as those suggested by Karen Yoshihara (1988):

1. Summarize your classmate's paper in one sentence. Your sentence should be your own version of a good topic sentence for his paper.

2. What did you like best about the way your classmate wrote his paper? Why? Be sure that you mention something that he can continue to do on future papers.

3. What are the three best questions to ask about your classmate's paper? If you don't have three good questions, you should have three separate comments about what you liked best (number 2, above) and at least one question.

Conclusion

The major assumptions we operate under when we teach writing are

❑ We learn to write by writing.

❑ All writing must be done for real purposes with real audiences.

Writing is an important part of the school day. Writers learn by interacting with print and by experimenting with thoughts and forms, without being forced to worry about correctness. Younger or newer ESL learners should not be excluded from writing merely because they have not yet mastered orthography, sentence patterns, or a large vocabulary. They need to be allowed to practice communicating thoughts, expressing feelings, and learning how to organize their thoughts on paper through the process of writing whole texts. Spelling and grammar will be learned during the act of writing. By providing a print environment with an attitude of acceptance for each student's attempts, you can help them grow as writers.

SPEAKING AND LISTENING

7

Chapter 3, "Students and Teachers," included a detailed discussion of ways in which the teacher can provide input that is both meaningful and useful to the second language learner. **In this chapter, we will look further at the listening and speaking components of acquiring a language. We will focus on**

- **Phases of language acquisition and what these look like in the classroom**

- **How to treat errors**

- **Developing the skill of listening—an end in itself**

Franco, who took his name from a Franco American truck driving by when he and his brother were choosing new American names, was twelve when he arrived from Taiwan and was enrolled in junior high. His family owned a Chinese restaurant in a nearby shopping mall. Although Barb (his ESL teacher, who worked with him three afternoons a week) and his classroom teachers were conscientious and patient, Franco's progress seemed very slow. Conversations with him were usually one way; he seldom managed more than a phrase or two here and there. More often than not, his response was either a shrug or an "I don't know." He could not do the regular work in his content area classes. He hardly seemed to be learning at all.

And yet outside the classroom, things were different. He consistently beat Barb at Monopoly and Risk. These are by no means easy games, and Barb explained the rules painstakingly in English. When they played Monopoly at the end of each session, they each kept their own property and money so that they could continue the next session where they had left off.

Barb would read out the Chance and the Community Chest cards that Franco drew, and more often than not he could follow the instructions without further explanation.

Although he was not a break-in artist, Franco gained the respect and admiration of the eighth-grade boys by demonstrating that he could open any combination lock in the school. Another demonstration of his ability to understand was when the other students would tell him, "Go tell Mrs. Mitchell, 'F_____ you.' " And with a wide grin on his face, Franco would obligingly go to Mrs. Mitchell and say, "F_____ you, Mrs. Mitchell," to the howls of his classmates.

Franco was a lot smarter and knew a lot more than he let on. He used his English (and his lack of it!) to his advantage, by selectively misunderstanding what he didn't feel like doing, by pretending he didn't know what he was saying, but clearly comprehending things that were important to him, such as the rules of games and instructions from classmates.

As with reading and writing, competence in both speaking and listening is best acquired in a natural setting. The environment Franco was immersed in was conducive to learning. He was not isolated in a language lab, learning "Hello, Mrs. Mitchell, how are you?" and "Please pass the pencils." He was surrounded by people using English for real purposes—to further relationships, to get homework done, to harass poor Mrs. Mitchell. Franco was strongly motivated to make friends and used the language skills he had to further that end. Having him spend his time working on pronunciation and grammar would not have helped much.

For second-language learners, our priority as teachers should be "fluency before accuracy." Getting things done supersedes getting things right. As they gain competence and confidence, students will work out the details of grammar and pronunciation.

To develop competency in both the listening and speaking areas of English, newcomers need

- **Teachers who understand the stages of acquisition and adjust their input to fit each student's level**

- **Teachers who are tolerant of errors, enabling students to learn without being labeled or punished for their pronunciation or word-choice errors**

- **Many opportunities to talk, listen, and interact with others**

Language Acquisition and Classroom Input

While acquiring a language is an individual process, we can make generalizations about the phases the learner goes through. A major "given" with language learning is that "comprehension precedes production." What Franco, for instance, said—or was able to say—was by no means indicative of the learning that was taking place. He could understand the complex rules of Monopoly, and while he would never have been able to explain them back, he could certainly follow the directions well enough to win time and again.

We see this with our own children learning their first language. Children recognize their names at five months, and phrases such as "Here's your Mom," and "Wave bye-bye" at about seven months, long before they say their first word. By the time they speak, they have had nearly a year of listening, and their ability to understand spoken messages far exceeds their ability to produce.

Researchers Burt and Dulay (1982) have found that language learners progress through three general stages as they gain communication skills. These are not necessarily discrete stages, they represent more of a continuum from no language to full participation:

THE THREE STAGES — A CONTINUUM

STAGE 1. One-way communication. The learner listens to the target language, but is not able to speak it.

A common question we hear from teachers is, "My student isn't saying anything. What can I do to make him talk?" Some researchers, such as Stephen Krashen (1983), claim that language learners go through a silent period, which can last between one and six months. Others have questioned this idea and found the time frame to be closer to two weeks. Still others say there is no such thing. But we have found that teachers will often tell us of students who have been in their classes for weeks without saying a word, leading them to believe that these students aren't learning.

This silent period can be caused by several things, or a combination of things. It could be a period of silent non-comprehension in which the new language simply seems like a stream of sound. It could be due to psychological withdrawal as a result of culture shock. Or it could simply be due to a particular student's personality; perhaps he is a shy person. The student's learning style could affect his production. This student may prefer to learn by rote memorization of rules, remaining silent until a number of structures are learned, rather than relying on intuitive knowledge and making the most of the skills he has already acquired. He may have come from a school in which asking questions indicates misunderstanding, an insult to the teacher, and a dishonorable thing to do.

Whether your students are silent for six months or begin to communicate the first day, they need to be allowed "listening time" without being forced to speak. Research has shown that the emphasis in learning a new language should be on listening first, and that forcing a student to speak can be detrimental to his learning. Granted, waiting until your student is ready to speak can be difficult. Going day after day speaking to a student who doesn't respond is frustrating; the temptation to force this student to say something—*anything!*—just to see if you are getting through can be strong. It may be easier to resist the temptation if you are aware that this is a passing stage.

STAGE 2. Partial two-way communication. The learners listen to the communication, respond either with gestures or in their native languages.

Students can demonstrate comprehension in ways other than speech. Allow them to respond by nodding their heads, pointing, drawing, gesturing, or pantomiming.

STAGE 3. Full two-way communication. The learners listen and respond effectively in the target language.

Research has revealed that people first learn a language in chunks. Their first utterances consist of unanalyzed wholes, such as "What's the matter?" or "That's mine." What these chunks do is allow a learner to participate in a conversation or game without having completely mastered the grammar of the language. From these chunks, they can move toward complete sentences as they figure out the rules of the new language.

Burt and Dulay state that these phases of language acquisition are important for the classroom teacher to understand for several reasons:

□ By understanding these stages you won't be overly concerned if your students' production does not match their ability to understand.

□ Students are able to succeed best if the level of activity matches their current stage of development. Therefore, if your students are capable of uttering only simple sentences, use activities that require minimal language skills.

FOUR LEVELS OF QUESTIONING   In chapter 3, "Students and Teachers," we discussed ways of adjusting your speech to make it easier for your students to understand. Good questioning techniques also encourage the students to respond in English, at their own levels. Here are four levels of questioning with some examples:

LEVEL 1. The teacher asks questions that require only *yes* or *no* answers. For example: "Are you standing?" "Can you hear me?" "Did Maria open the window?"

LEVEL 2. The teacher asks either/or questions, and the students respond with one-word answers using either a noun or a verb. For example: "Are you walking or standing?" "Is she sitting on the table or on the chair?"

LEVEL 3. The teacher asks questions using *where* or *what*, and the students are able to respond with a single word or a partial phrase. For example: "Where is Baldo sitting?" Answer: "On the floor." "What is Rocio doing?" "Sitting."

LEVEL 4. The teacher uses no content vocabulary to ask questions, and the students are able to respond in full sentences. For example: "What is Sabina doing?" "She's dancing." "What will Salvador do?" "He's going to shut the door." "What did Anna do?" "She climbed on the chair."

This hierarchy of questions is an important concept to remember. In the teacher's rush to communicate, it is easy to overlook the complexity of question-asking. Yet, questions that are above the students' comprehension levels can be confusing for them. When the students' problem is the grammar used, not the vocabulary, rephrasing the question often creates more confusion. For example, you might start out with the question: "What time is it?" Then when the students fail to understand, you may try rephrasing the question, "What time do you *think* it is?" or "What do the hands on the clock say?" believing that stating it another way might help. If the students understood the concept, however, they would have been able to answer the question in the first place. If they didn't, rephrasing would only confuse them further, because they are hearing *three* questions they don't understand, not one. If the students are confused at one level of questioning, revert to the previous one. For example, if the student doesn't understand "Where are you going?" revert to "Are you going home or to Mrs. Smith's class?"

Tolerance for Errors

Perfect comprehension and production are not realistic goals for second-language learners. Students need to be encouraged to express themselves, and a casual attitude towards oral mistakes, in which one accepts all attempts at communication and does not pounce on errors, will foster confidence and the willingness to speak up. However, this doesn't mean ignoring them altogether.

Grammatical and pronunciation errors often *do* get in the way of communication, and the goal, if not to eradicate a foreign accent, is to move the student toward speech that a listener does not have to struggle to understand.

My students make a lot of mistakes in grammar. Should I correct them or not?

GRAMMATICAL ERRORS

Just as we discussed in the chapters on reading and writing, emphasize communication and meaning, not correctness. Most parents recognize that acquiring language is a process that takes several years. A two-year-old does not come out with perfectly formed grammatical sentences. His speech is apt to be limited to only one or two words, such as "Mommy, juice," or "big dog." Instead of looking for mistakes, parents focus on the meaning and content of the child's speech. They are confident that these "mistakes" will disappear in time as the child matures and communicates. Parents don't correct their children for their linguistic inaccuracies. If a child says "Daddy goed to work," the mother accepts this as communication and responds to the truth of the statement. However, if a child points to a dog and says "cat," the mother will correct this error in fact. Parents will also use correct language in response, thereby "modeling" correct usage.

As teachers, however, we often feel that it is our responsibility to point out errors. We feel constrained to correct every mistake the student makes, feeling that if we don't, the student will continue to make that error.

If we view second-language learning as a process that takes a number of years, and recognize that students need time to hone and refine the rules of our language, we can view these mistakes not as faults, but as stages of development the students have reached on their way to mastering English. Whatever they say, and however they say it, we need to recognize, understand, appreciate, and nurture their attempts to communicate by responding to the message.

Research has shown that pointing out mistakes seems to do very little for language learners and may serve more to distract them from their meaning than help them get meaning across. Pointing out mistakes may even impede their progress, because this approach focuses more on form than on meaning, and also undermines their confidence in their attempts to communicate.

Krashen advises that the focus of language should be on communication, not on grammatical structure. So as you observe your students relax and begin to make attempts at communication with you and with other students, encourage them to move beyond silence and focus on continued language interaction. This focus relieves you of the expectations that students must produce "perfect English." The students then have the opportunity to make their own generalizations, and gradually, through time, practice, and the process of error-making will come to approximate the English they hear spoken around them every day.

Use errors as benchmarks to a student's progress, and use your knowledge of these errors for subjects to work on at other times. We discuss in chapter 4, "Whole Language Learning and the Four Skills," how to use patterned language to focus on specifics such as tenses. Another option is to give brief mini-lessons on these specifics during the editing stages of writing.

Modeling, as parents do, is another way of giving students input about their speech. For instance, if Lupe says, "I no like broccoli," you can respond with, "Oh, you don't like broccoli. What *do* you like?" Thus, she can hear the correct form in the context of a statement that has immediate relevance to her.

If a student has expressly stated the wish to have his grammar corrected then it is best to do so, but only *after* he has finished talking. You can say, "You said 'losted.' The correct form is 'lost.' " But make these corrections only if invited. The long-term efficacy of corrections is dubious, and usually only satisfies the individual student's need to know.

We want to emphasize that error correction is not a one-shot solution; you cannot correct or work on an error once and expect the student never to make the same error again. Sorting out the grammar of a language is a long slow process. For this reason, we reiterate that a lenient attitude toward errors in grammar is the wisest course to follow while the students sort out the intricacies of grammar for themselves.

My students have difficulties with pronunciation. Shouldn't I work on these?

Pronunciation is another matter altogether. While we still advocate that getting something said is more important than getting it right, there are times when you may have to take steps to help a student with pronunciation.

TROUBLE WITH PRONUNCIATION

A controversy exists among authorities in second-language learning as to whether or not this is important. Many experts feel that the language learner will correct pronunciation problems later in the acquisition process. However, others—ourselves included—believe that some language learners are not able to do this. Frequently, students whose native language has tones (such as Chinese, Vietnamese, or Thai) or a different stress and pitch system, have great difficulty speaking English that can be easily understood. Because they respond to tones, in speaking they often drop the endings of words. For example, "You like some bread?" will sound like "You li' so' brea'?" or "His wife is at home," will sound like "Hi' wi' a' ho'." The focus for teaching pronunciation should be on helping the students to communicate—to get their meaning across accurately—not on the correct reproduction of minimal pairs (sounds produced in the same place in the mouth, in the same way, but that nevertheless differ, such as *p/b*, *f/v*).

Every language uses a certain number of sounds to make up words, and they are not always the same. Some languages have sounds we don't have. Spanish, for instance has two *r*'s, the rolled *r* in *perro*, and the *r* in *pero*. Farsi and German have the guttural *h* as in *khoshamedi* and *ich*. Other languages don't have sounds that we have, or "hear" only one sound where we hear two. Arabic speakers, for instance, do not distinguish between *p* and *b*; Spanish speakers don't distinguish between *sh* and *ch*. The Navajo language doesn't distinguish between *p*, *b*, and *m*. Often these speakers cannot hear the difference.

Differences are not only confined to different languages, but different dialects within a language as well. In her speech, Mary, a Northern California native, doesn't distinguish the difference between the vowel sounds in *cot* (kät) and *caught* (kôt). To Barb, from the Midwest, this is incomprehensible. Barb can hear it; why can't Mary? How pointless it would be for Barb to stop everything and drill Mary in this difference! If Barb said, "I was sleeping on a cot in the tent when my husband caught two fish on Lake Oroville," no one would have any doubt about which word Barb was using when. To label Mary as stupid or slow because she can't hear the difference would be ridiculous. And yet this has been done time and again to students whose dialects or languages do not contain certain sounds we use in our own dialect. One of Barb's student teachers, for example, discovered that the students he was tutoring couldn't distinguish between *f* and *v*, and spent an entire week helping them articulate the different sounds. Drilling them endlessly on sounds they cannot distinguish is pointless, and more often than not extremely frustrating. What's more, in the face of the whole task of learning English, it is a waste of time.

But we must address the problems created when students speak English structures correctly, but still have problems being understood because of their pronunciation. Mary had a student, Thien, who went to a fast-food restaurant and ordered "free hamburgers." He immediately got a lecture on how "We work for things in this country; if you think you're here for a handout, then go back where you came from." What Thien really meant to order was *three* hamburgers, but as he was not able to articulate the aspirated *th*, he was misunderstood. This particular sound is difficult for students of many language backgrounds. These students compensate by using *f* or *t* in the place of *th*.

Working with minimal pairs within the context of words, for example, *hit* versus *heat*, *free* versus *three*, *very* versus *berry* is often not very productive, but it can work more effectively if the minimal pair work is part of a natural sentence structure. Try using as examples idioms that students find useful or puzzling and want to know the meaning of, such as "save your brea*th*" and "*th*rough *th*ick and *th*in," or common phrases like "*Th*anks a lot."

Mary found that it was helpful to alert students to the problems they would encounter when trying to pronounce English. Some students preferred to be told that it would be difficult for them to say certain sounds; they then were able to spell, write, draw, and so on in order to communicate.

Pronunciation is more complex than simply mastering minimal pairs. Students from other countries often have a difficult time with the stress and pitch system in the English sentence. As a result, these students can often sound angry, excited, or emphatic to a native-English speaker, when to their own ears they are being solicitous and polite.

Another facet of pronunciation that eludes many ESL students is the clipped, de-emphasized English spoken in informal conversation (often referred to as "reduced English") in which we drop endings and slur our words together. Mary once spent a period of time with her students explaining the *have + to* (*hafta*) construction, when one of her students asked, "When are we going to learn about *gotta*?" Imagine how frustrating this type of language is to the students who, when speaking in their own language, were rewarded for consistent clarity!

Activities to help improve the students' sensitivity to the nuances of English can be enjoyable. Focus the students' attention on listening to differences in pitch patterns by comparing the pronunciation of words that occur in several languages, like *chocolate* or *coffee*. Have the students pronounce their names with you, pronouncing them the way North Americans would tend to. This helps them focus on the differences in pitch or minimal sounds. Sometimes students discover that a word they have heard frequently but didn't understand is actually a North American approximation of their names!

As you can see, we believe that drilling on sounds in isolation is counterproductive; pointing out troublesome sounds and having the student practice them within words is more helpful. Work on pronunciation only when the students express a wish to focus on improving their language "delivery" or when their pronunciation of certain words gets in the way of being understood.

Opportunities to Talk and Listen

ESL learners need to interact with the English language in order to strengthen their skills. Elsewhere we discuss cooperative learning techniques. In this section, we will give suggestions for activities you can use to increase the students' speaking and listening competency.

We feel it is important to promote listening as an end in itself, not merely as a means to speaking. We spend much of our time listening; we listen to conversations, radio, TV, and so on. Listening is a critical skill for a language learner to grasp, particularly in the content classes where sophisticated listening skills are demanded, such as when following directions in a science lab; or when listening to lectures in history and government, to rules in phys. ed., or to explanations of procedures in math.

Here are some strategies you can use to promote listening and speaking skills.

TPR—TOTAL PHYSICAL RESPONSE

"Total Physical Response," developed by James Asher (1982), is one of the richest and most successful activities you can use. It can involve one student or the entire class. You can turn the responsibility for this activity over to an aide, a native-English speaker, or even a proficient student. The underlying premise is that listening and understanding English language must come before the actual attempt to speak. The strategy is based upon the belief that language acquisition can be greatly accelerated through the use of body movement; therefore each lesson includes commands and actions that help the student learn through doing. By listening and responding physically to instructions or commands, students are involved to a greater extent than when they respond only verbally. In the relaxed fun atmosphere of a TPR lesson, students learn very quickly and efficiently. In TPR, students are not required to respond orally, they are simply asked to follow the directions given by the teacher.

A typical TPR lesson proceeds as follows:

1. The teacher gives a command, modeling if necessary. For instance, say "Stand up," at the same time standing up yourself. Remember to speak in a normal tone of voice at normal speed.

Do not speak too slowly or the students will quickly become bored and inattentive.

2. Students respond physically by standing up. Slower learners can watch and imitate the actions of others who have caught on more quickly.

3. When a number of commands have been given and learned, you can combine them to form a series. For example, "Mario, stand up, walk to the window, and open it."

As students pass through the stages of acquisition, and their ability to speak English develops, TPR gives them the opportunity to take control and use their newly acquired vocabulary by acting as the TPR leader. You can now have *them* give the series of commands to the class, motivating them to speak clearly and enunciate correctly. You can use this time to pinpoint pronunciation problems your students might have. You have a natural opportunity for working on strengthening those points within a meaningful context.

Use TPR to introduce important survival verbs such as *walk*, *go*, *stop*, *turn*, *close*, *open*, *lock*, *unlock*, *sit*, *stand*. You can embed other important vocabulary within the commands in sentences such as, "Francisco, pick up the blue book and put it under the fire extinguisher."

TPR is primarily a listening activity, but can become a very rich and enjoyable activity involving *all* of the four language-arts skills. Language learners are helped to make the speech–print connection if, once a series of commands is mastered, you write the series on the board for students to read and, if possible, copy for themselves. Realizing that the words they have just heard and responded to are the words they now see on the board is an important step.

If you find that your high school students are reticent about marching around the classroom, or you think that the TPR activities described above would not be appropriate in your class, then adapt TPR to your specific situation. If you are working with a small group of students within a larger class setting, try working with manipulables. For example, place cut-outs of a square, circle, diamond, star, and triangle in front of the group of students. Point to a shape and say, "This is a star. Now *you* point to the star." Do the same with one other shape, then review with the star. As the students understand what you are doing, you can have them vary the activity by picking up the shapes and giving them to each other. You can expand this activity to a string of directions in which they listen to your commands and draw the shapes on a piece of paper. For example: "Draw a star in the upper right-hand corner, draw a triangle in the middle," and so on. Then have them circle, underline, check, or cross out the items they put on the paper. You then show the students a model of your instructions, repeating what you said so they can check their papers to see if they followed the instructions correctly. The students are learning listening skills without having to respond verbally. They are also learning to follow a sequence of directions with vocabulary they will be expected to know.

You can use these types of modifications in the content areas, such as science and math, to help students learn to follow instructions or master basic vocabulary. Have your regular students model the appropriate actions. Pair a newcomer with a native-English speaker when following maps or a procedure in science.

GAMES   Use games to review content area knowledge. Games are very useful for encouraging student participation and, ultimately, language growth. Best of all, with games, the focus is on the activity, not on language structure. Here are some easily adaptable games:

❑   **Bingo.** This game, played with words instead of numbers, is appropriate for all levels and all classes, since it focuses on important vocabulary. Have each student list vocabulary words on prepared grids much like bingo cards. Have another student pull the same vocabulary words, which have been written on slips of paper, out of a bag and read them out loud. The students then cover the words on their grids with slips of paper, poker chips, kidney beans, or some other token. The object of the game is to see who gets *bingo* first.

❑   **Go Fish.** This game is good for reviewing content vocabulary by matching pictures and new vocabulary, or simply using the picture-matching method to require students to supply the vocabulary words from memory when shown the pictures. You can make the game cards out of index cards. If you do not have the time, have an aide, a native-English speaker, or even an ESL student make the cards. You can use this game as an ice breaker for new students, because, along with the vocabulary, students can learn each other's names in a relaxed setting.

❑   **Categories.** In this game, have students write a word relevant to a particular topic across the top or down the side of a page. The students must then list words that can be categorized beside each letter of the topic. For example, a lesson in nutrition could require the students to think of words from the category of food to fill in beside the words "good health."

G	grapes	H	ham
O	oranges	E	eggs
O	onions	A	apples
D	dim sum	L	limes
		T	turkey
		H	hamburger

This activity is a lot of fun when done as a group. It can last as long as the students can think of words to fit into each column. This exercise works best when the topic word has a variety of letters and when the category the students use to find the words is very general.

❑ **Hangman or Password.** Always favorites with students, these are good games for vocabulary review and also help reinforce spelling. They can be played with either simple or difficult words.

❑ **Memory.** For about two minutes, show the class a detailed picture of a place or an event, or a tray filled with items. After the students have studied the picture or tray, remove or cover it and ask questions about the contents to see how much they remembered. (How many cats were in the picture? What color was the one by the door? What was next to the spool of thread? How many crayons were on the tray?) Or have children draw the objects, labeling them when they know the words.

- **Interviews.** Make a list of about twenty statements. Draw a line in front of each statement. For example:

  _____ has been to Disneyland.

  _____ wears glasses.

  _____ has a sister.

  Have the students interview each other to find out whose name(s) is/are appropriate for each blank. Set a time limit for this activity. Students enjoy finding things out about each other and have an opportunity to use English in the process.

- **Silent films.** With silent films, students do not need to struggle with language to understand what is going on; this is a purely visual experience. After viewing a film, the students respond to questions about it. If showing an action film, stop the projector at a critical turning point in the plot, and ask students to suggest their own preferred endings, orally and/or in writing. You can use these activities with beginning, intermediate, and advanced students.

- **Tongue Twisters.** Students enjoy tackling the old favorites such as "She sells seashells by the seashore," "Peter Piper picked a peck of pickled peppers," "How much wood could a woodchuck chuck if a woodchuck could chuck wood?" or "Rubber baby buggy bumpers."

Conclusion

The major assumptions we operate under concerning speaking and listening are

- Learners acquire language in an environment that is full of talk that invites response.

- Students will speak when they are ready.

- Fluency precedes accuracy.

- An acceptance of all attempts, whether correct or incorrect, will promote confidence.

Provide opportunities for the students to develop these skills. Present lessons consisting of content that is meaningful, while asking questions appropriate for the students' level, in an atmosphere that encourages students to take risks. The interaction you encourage allows for language experimentation and, ultimately, leads to language acquisition.

CONTENT AREA INSTRUCTION 8

In this chapter, we will discuss some of the problems ESL students face in content-area classes and give suggestions on

□   Modifying textbooks

□   Organizing material

□   Presenting lessons in an organized, comprehensible way

Content area learning begins in earnest in the upper elementary grades. From the fourth grade onward, sometimes earlier, students are not "just learning to read" anymore, they are being required to read to learn. They must have the requisite fluency and skills in reading, and the background knowledge required to gather information from a text. Because many of our non-English-speaking students come to us with poor reading skills and many gaps in the kind of background knowledge that we take for granted with our mainstream students, these requirements pose special problems for teachers of the upper elementary grades. The problems are even more acute for those junior high and high school teachers who specialize in one subject.

In recent years, the influx of non-native speakers has been high. One school district in California, for example, saw its enrollment almost doubled from three hundred and fifty to six hundred students over one summer. The majority of these students were Hmong. Neither the budget nor the classrooms were large enough to accommodate such a large influx, and teachers found their classes overflowing. Students were mainstreamed, ready or not. For want of better placements, newcomers found themselves placed in such inappropriate classes as French and Spanish. By the middle of October, a myriad of problems had set in: the students couldn't do the work; frustrated by their inability to communicate with their peers, much less keep up with class work, they were becoming behavior problems; the teachers felt overwhelmed by the dual task of teaching native-English speakers and trying to teach students who not only did not know English but who were barely literate.

This might sound familiar. Out of a class of twenty-five, many teachers throughout North America—particularly in inner-city urban classrooms—have seven or more ESL students. Because of the limited human and financial resources available, these students may have been given only a year of specialized ESL instruction and then mainstreamed, even though they were far from proficient in English. As a teacher, you have a curriculum to cover and eighteen students who can do the work and can't wait around while you spend all your time trying to help the ESL students.

As we have noted before, many believe that ESL students should learn English first, and only when they have enough oral proficiency, begin content area learning in earnest. One supervisor recently visited the high school English classroom of one of her student teachers. In the back of the room sat Khae, a Southeast Asian student. Khae was not given anything to do and did not participate in classroom activities. The supervisor asked why he was not included. The student teacher's reply was that she had been told by the school counselor that she didn't have to worry about trying to include him until he had learned English. (How this was supposed to happen had nothing to do with her!)

Imagine Khae's progress. He is allowed a year of oral development: listening, speaking, working on his language competence. If all goes well, within that year he might speak fairly well, be able to communicate his needs, relate to his friends, and produce a passable English sentence. Along the way, he might have begun reading and may even be able to write a few sentences. He might have been promoted to the next grade.

In the meantime, his classmates are reading and writing at grade level, taking the content classes such as history, geography, math, and science required for graduation from high school. As the years progress, Khae will be left further and further behind. The gap in background knowledge will become wider; study skills will not be learned. The lag is cumulative; as success breeds success, so too does failure breed failure.

INTEGRATING LANGUAGE AND CONTENT

This scenario does not have to—and should not—happen. Recent research has shown that students can learn content and language at the same time. In fact, we know that integrating language and content—learning the content material and the language needed to understand the content at the same time—is more effective than simply learning language and only then trying to learn content. There are several important reasons for this:

- **Integrated instruction brings both cognitive development and language development together.**

- **Content provides real meaning,** not just structures of language that are abstractions and may seem to be of little value to the learner.

- **When students are learning subject and language together they are more motivated because the content is interesting and valuable to them.**

- **The language used in school is different from the language used outside the classroom.** James Cummins (1980) distinguishes between basic interpersonal communication skills (BICS) and cognitive-academic language proficiency (CALP). Within a year or two, a student might have mastered the BICS. He might be a competent speaker, have friends, and be able to carry on conversations in English. But while these interpersonal communication skills are important, they are not enough to succeed in school. For several reasons they do not carry over into the content areas where other kinds of language demands are made.

  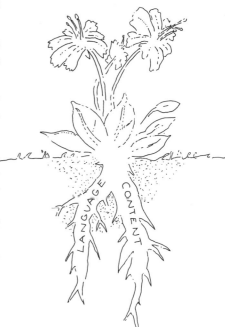

  - Basic interpersonal communication skills are inadequate to attain the higher-level skills of problem solving, inferring, analyzing, synthesizing, and predicting—skills required for academic success in the content areas.

  - Conversations are embedded in meaningful context. Students can pick up clues (body language, gestures, facial expressions) to gain meaning. They can also ask for clarification if they don't understand. But academic language is usually "context reduced"; a student is often asked to obtain information by reading texts that have few pictures to help guide comprehension. Cummins suggests that these cognitive academic skills (CALP) require five to seven years to acquire.

Many of your students come out of ESL or bilingual programs with good oral skills, but have either undeveloped academic language skills or need help transferring to English the knowledge they have acquired using their native languages.

Potential Problems

The academic language of content area classes can pose many problems for ESL students. Knowing what these problems are will help your students bridge the gap between their first language and the linguistic demands of the lesson. Students in content-area classes are likely to have problems in the following areas: vocabulary, syntax, and pragmatics.

WITH VOCABULARY
- Each subject has its own particular set of terms that the students may not yet have learned, such as *synthesis, microorganism, abolitionist, impeach, coeffient, addend*.

- Many words used in everyday language have a specialized meaning within specific content areas, such as *product* or *square* in math, *kingdom* and *energy* in science, or *primary* and *inflation* in social studies.

- Many words are abstract and can't be explained simply, for example, *democracy, justice*.

WITH SYNTAX
- Textbooks commonly use the passive voice, reversing the normal word order, a form students come to understand and use only later on in their acquisition of English. For example, "This polarization is reinforced by the mass of contradictory evidence that seems to lend support to both sides." (Many native-English speakers will have trouble with that one!)

  Texts often use complex sentences whose meanings hinge on transition words like *because* or *although*, which students may not understand or notice, for example, "Both the Puritans and the Pilgrims left England because they felt the Anglican Church should become more like the Catholic Church," or "Although her business was unfinished, she left."

WITH PRAGMATICS
- With pragmatics (involving the larger units of discourse, beyond the word, phrase, and sentence level, such as the text itself and your lectures)
  - Students may not have enough English proficiency to understand the textbook or your lectures.
  - They may not know how to read difficult material for various purposes or have strong enough study skills to extract information from their textbook or reference materials. Many times they read narratives the same way they read expository prose, or editorials as if they were facts.
  - They may not have the general knowledge we assume with our North American students. For example, they may not understand the concept of democracy, or the meaning of ecosystems; or may be unfamiliar with animals such as mountain lions and armadillos; or they may not have learned of the Challenger space shuttle.

Bridging the Gap

A typical period in a traditional content area classroom consists of a lecture, discussion of the assigned textbook readings with students, then tests based on these lectures and readings. Until they achieve full proficiency in English for academic purposes, ESL students simply cannot succeed in such circumstances.

This does not mean they are doomed to failure. There are ways in which students *can* succeed in content area classes. They can learn language *through* language. In other words, they do not need to learn English by learning it formally as an isolated activity; they can learn subject matter if they can follow and understand the lesson. The subject matter then becomes the vehicle for language acquisition. **Your goals are**

1. **To help your students learn English.** They need to learn the specialized vocabulary of your particular discipline as well as be given the opportunity to learn such skills as explaining, informing, describing, classifying, and evaluating.

2. **To teach your content area.**

3. **To teach the higher-level thinking skills.**

4. **To promote literacy.** No longer is teaching reading and writing solely the job of the English teacher. These teaching skills belong in every classroom where students need help in understanding lectures, making presentations, reading for information, and writing reports.

YOUR GOALS

What to Do

The big challenge is to make the content area lessons comprehensible, meeting the needs of both your regular students *and* your ESL students—challenging the native-English speakers while making content meaningful and accessible to the others.

It *can* be done. The following strategies will help not only your ESL students, but will also enrich learning for your regular students. Strategies to make content easier for ESL students often achieve the same result with *all* students. Again, good teaching is good teaching, and good teaching techniques are especially important for teachers of ESL students.

You can embed content within meaningful context by involving all four language-arts skills—reading, writing, listening, and speaking—in active ways. Strategies include grouping, modifying textbooks, and setting priorities.

When you're faced with ESL students and hardly know where to begin, it's easy to get bogged down in the day-to-day problems and lose sight of the overall picture. Here are some steps to help you manage:

BEFORE YOU TEACH ■ **Develop a plan.** If you have established an overall plan for the course as we suggested in chapter 1, "First Days," you are way ahead of the game. You have goals for your students, competencies they must develop to succeed, and themes to build the course around so that with each successive spiral, the students better understand the material. Now you can go on and work out the fine points of your particular subject matter.

■ **Analyze the textbook.** You may or may not use a textbook. For many classes a textbook is the main resource for classroom learning, and reading this book is integral to understanding the content of the course. But what you expect when you say, "Read the following pages for tomorrow's class" and what your students actually *do* are often very different. For this reason we discuss the use of textbooks, including some strategies for modifying the text to meet the needs of your students.

You can't take for granted that the students in your class have either adequate study skills or sufficient language proficiency to meet the objectives you have laid out for them. Many students, English speakers included, are poor readers and have poor study skills. Many texts assume that students are all reading on grade level, which often is not true of ESL students (nor of many others!) They may take the book home, they may not; they may skim it with comprehension, or they may read every word and still not understand what they have read.

When reviewing a textbook, consider the following points:

❑ Does the subject matter covered match the priorities you have set? When you check this match, decide what to cover and what you will be able to gloss over. If a chapter or section doesn't fit into your scheme, skip it.

❑ Analyze the textbook from the ESL students' viewpoint. What problems might your students have? What concepts and vocabulary might be new and unfamiliar to them?

Textbooks presume a great deal of background knowledge. For instance, most North Americans know a lot of history. We may not know all the facts behind historical incidents, but most of us have a general idea of our history; we have watched countless westerns, mini-series, and dramas on television and in films, trudged through museums, and visited historical sites on field trips.

We cannot, however, presume this background knowledge on the part of ESL students. Many of these students from other countries were extremely successful in school and have rich experiences to bring to the learning task. Others know of nothing outside their refugee camp or their village. Knowledge of their native country's role in world affairs may be non-existent, much less knowledge of the history of the U.S. or Canada.

But they *do* understand the concept of immigration and change. Many have firsthand knowledge of war, many are now experiencing cultural conflict and the challenge of adjusting to new technology and new ways to make a living. They all understand the concept of freedom. These are critical issues in their lives. You can capitalize on these things, by using what they *do* know as a starting base.

- **Identify essential vocabulary**. Every subject has its own special content vocabulary. For example, the words *population, community, ecosystem, biosphere, tissue, cells* are fundamental vocabulary to science. This is vocabulary you cannot simplify and which must be specifically taught. Students need to know these words to read the text and to go on to more specialized or broader knowledge in that particular field.

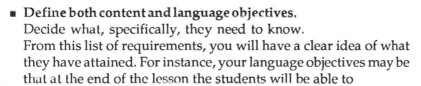

- **Define both content and language objectives**.
  Decide what, specifically, they need to know.
  From this list of requirements, you will have a clear idea of what they have attained. For instance, your language objectives may be that at the end of the lesson the students will be able to

  - Understand the essential vocabulary for this unit

  - Write a report of their findings

  - Present findings orally

  Your content objectives may be that students

  - Practice observation and recording skills

  - Research a particular component of the unit

  - Demonstrate understanding of information presented by other students

- **Organize the material into small, easily attainable and sequential steps**. You can organize your lesson in a structured way so that you can teach study skills at the same time as content. We demonstrate how in the next section.

WHEN YOU TEACH   Expanding on the familiar "preview, view, and review" format, Chamot and O'Malley (1987), who developed the Cognitive Academic Language Learning Approach, suggest the following five steps:

1. Prepare
2. Present
3. Practice
4. Evaluate
5. Follow-up

Follow the same procedure for each segment or unit. If, for instance, your next unit of study is recycling garbage, you may want to proceed in the following way, using any or all of the suggestions under each heading.

- **Prepare.** Like pre-reading and pre-writing, this stage "primes the pump," focusing students' attention on the topic, getting them to think about it and make connections between what they already know and what they have not yet learned.

  □ **Announce the global theme of the lesson.** Give the students a short summary, or read the chapter summary aloud.

  □ **Go on a field trip** to the local recyclers, or go out for a walk. Choose a strip of land near the school or adjacent to a fast food restaurant to see how much and how many different kinds of garbage can be found.

  □ **Tap the students' prior knowledge; find out how much they know about the subject before the lesson.** By doing this you can get a fair idea of how much vocabulary and background knowledge you need to teach, and how much you can assume. One way to do this is to have a brainstorming session in which small groups of three write down all the words they can think of on the topic.

  □ **Help them organize their thoughts** by mapping their ideas. Mapping is a way to plan, organize, and structure ideas and their supporting facts. It is an exercise similar to outlining, but shows the relationships among ideas rather than simply listing them. Here are the steps involved in mapping:

    Place the main idea—Things We Throw Away—in the center of the page (or the blackboard, if you are doing this together.)

    Branch out with associated or connected ideas or examples. Use only key words.

    Continue to branch out from your associated ideas with supporting ideas—details. Again, use only key words.

Have them think about which of these items, can be recycled.

Ask them "What if..." or "What happens when..." questions, such as "What if we ran out of space for garbage dumps?" or "What happens when nobody recycles?" or "What happens to a diaper (or a kitchen stove or a banana) when it's thrown away?"

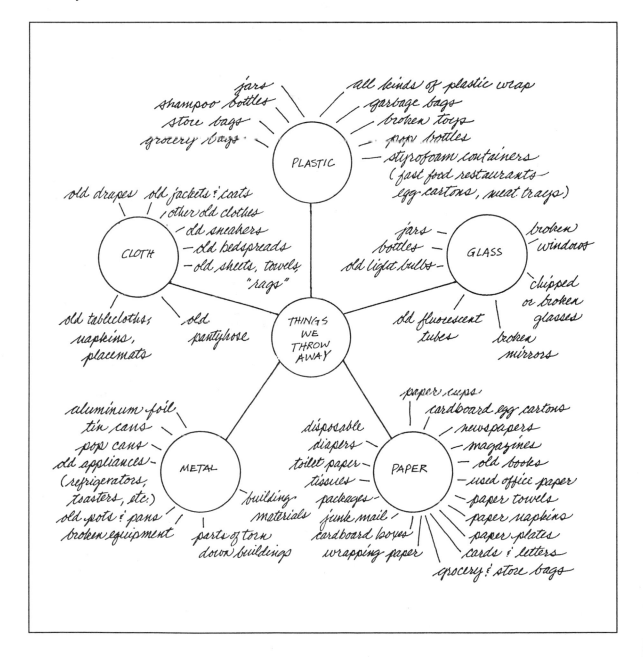

- **Teach difficult vocabulary.** Limit this to no more than twelve words. You need not teach every difficult word; many they can understand through the context. But before they read or begin the lesson, be sure they know and understand any terms essential to the topic.

- **Present.** On the board, outline or list the major concepts of the unit. This is a critical step for all students, not just your ESL students. Many regular students have poor note-taking and organizational skills. Putting a basic outline on the board will help them master the art of note-taking, plus give them a clear sense of what you think is important and what they need to learn.

  - **Present the new material.** You can do this in a variety of ways:

    Lecturing

    Showing a movie

    Demonstrating a process

    Playing a tape

    Imaginative use of overhead projectors, slide-tape presentations, simulations, and realia can not only enliven a class but reinforce your oral presentation. Use combinations of these, such as a lecture illustrated by photographs, maps, or dioramas; or demonstrate a process before assigning the reading.

  - **Explain the lesson, providing clear transitions and markers for key points** such as: *first, second, for instance, in conclusion.*

  - **Lead a brainstorming activity** to generate some of the dominant themes for students to research.

  - **Assign the text following your lesson.** It might not seem to make sense to assign the reading *after* the lecture, because you want the students to be able to come to class able to discuss the chapter, but the reality is that many will not. Students often wait until after the lecture because the readings contain so much information they have never encountered before that they are not able to understand it. Once you've covered the material in class, the students can read with a greater degree of understanding.

  - **Focus the students on the reading they are to do.** Give them something to look for, or to concentrate on. Most textbooks weigh all information equally, and unless you tell them, students will not know what is important. A critical part of reading at the upper grade levels is not only knowing what to pay attention to but what *not* to. Many students either laboriously read every word, or don't read at all, because they do not know which information they are supposed to be focusing on.

- ❑ **Use specific instructions when you assign the text,** such as, "People are finding it difficult to sort their garbage correctly when they take it to the recyclers. How has the plastics industry helped to solve that problem?"

- ❑ **Walk the students through the text**: read the title; study the pictures; read the first paragraph; point out the boldface type, the italics, maps, graphs, and pictures that are included to assist comprehension; read the last paragraph.

- ■ Practice. Have the students put into practice what you have presented, so that they can fully understand the concepts. Math and science teachers have always recognized that the way to master their subjects is by repeated practice—doing many similar problems and conducting experiments. This approach is critical to *all* the content areas. ESL students in particular need hands-on experience to cement the learning that is taking place. In the example of the unit on recycling garbage:

  - ❑ Catalog the categories and amount of garbage thrown away on the designated plot of land. Students can calculate how far away from the local McDonald's the wrappers begin to appear, and observe which ones get thrown out first.

  - ❑ Have each student study the garbage in their household for a specified period of time, recycle this garbage (newspapers, glass, plastic, and so on), and record their findings.

  - ❑ Investigate ways of using recycled material and their efficacy for the U.S. or Canada.

  - ❑ Set up a mini-recycling center for the school or the class.

- ■ **Evaluate their understanding.** After the students have had the opportunity to practice the new material in a meaningful way, you need to evaluate their understanding. This does not necessarily mean a test; you can assign a specific task instead. You can do any of the following:

  - ❑ Have students share their observations or their answers with each other.

  - ❑ Have students give short presentations on what they learned.

  - ❑ Have students write brief summaries of their notes to be exchanged with other students.

  - ❑ Have students write one thing they learned that day and one question still unanswered.

□ Have students map the text. You can use the results to check for understanding, or draw from them to formulate questions for exams. Students can explain their maps orally or work together to refine them. Go over what they have written down to add further details to the maps.

■ **Follow up.** So that students have a chance to integrate the new concepts with the old, plan some type of follow-up activity such as

□ Extensive reading about countries such as Japan, which have limited space and resources, thus making recycling a necessity.

□ Skits and role-plays: dialogues between recyclers and non-believers, between business and environmentalists.

□ Designing posters or writing ad campaigns.

□ Writing letters to federal or state/provincial political representatives or local officials to lobby for more stringent laws and recycling efforts.

□ Inviting a local official to speak to the class on the issue.

Testing for Mastery of Concepts

Testing is a tricky area. Sometimes students' ability to write in English makes it difficult to determine just how much they have learned. Or they may not have enough English proficiency to understand the question, even though they may well understand the concept.

CHECKING INFORMALLY FOR UNDERSTANDING

There are less stressful methods of evaluating student progress than tests. Many of the tasks you set in the evaluation section of each lesson can give you a more accurate picture of what each student knows. Here are some other informal means of checking for students' understanding:

■ **Observe their behavior** while they work and interact with others in the practice situation. Does Saif participate or does he sit back and let others take the initiative and do the work? Does Lupe make meaningful contributions? How often and how many? Does Shinsuke look lost and bewildered by the task?

■ **Talk with the students about their work.** Discuss what they've done. Often students are better able to articulate their understanding verbally than in writing.

■ **Examine the work they have produced.** Give credit for any input they have made, whether non-verbal or verbal.

If tests are an integral part of your course, here are some suggestions for making tests "easier" for the ESL student:

- **Consider giving the test orally.** Arrange for a bilingual parent or aide to interpret.

- **Simplify the language you use in the test.** Unless you are testing vocabulary that is important to your field of study, avoid words you have not taught.

- **Simplify the structures.** Make the instructions simple and give straightforward commands, such as "Complete the following." Avoid complex sentences.

- **Test only the specific skill or concept you have taught; don't test language.** For example, here is an answer to a test question given by eighth-grader Chantamala:

> *New world my father like to go to the new world because you can do everything like the way that know. We can go at the jungle, and cuting the wood to make a house, hunting, killing, growing crop or other thing that you wanted to do best for your life or family, then you can do everything that you want by your own.*

It is easy to get lost or overwhelmed by the errors in an ESL student's paper. At first glance the composition above might seem incoherent and disorganized, but the student has actually understood quite a bit of the discussion. The students were asked the question: "Would you like to move to the New World? Why? Give reasons." The class had just studied the colonization of America. This student gives very specific reasons why the New World was better. Even with her garbled language, she has conveyed the message that people could do anything they wanted: build their own homes, cut wood, kill animals—rights denied in many Old World countries. She has understood that the New World offered freedom from the harsh restricted life of common people in the Old World. If Chantamala were to be graded on her command of English, her many errors would count against her; however, she has learned some of the basic concepts and demonstrated her understanding of them.

Name _____

Date _____ Period ____

Briefly define or describe the following terms:

Sea Dogs *they were Sleves*

Golden Hind *siled th rayt the strait of magellan*

Charter *it document the rules*

Armada *a warship*

Joint Stock Company *a company*

House of Burgesses

Royal Colony *under complete control*

puritans *were reformers*

separatist *new churches*

pilgrims *or religious travelers*

Fundamental Orders *plans of the goven.*

proprietors *charters and own eq,*

patroons *religious groups*

Quakers

Frame of Government *gave the colonists a representative*

Pennsylvania Dutch *which means Germans*

Your criteria for grading might look like this:

☐ Did she understand the question?

☐ Did she answer the question?

☐ How well did she develop her thoughts?

☐ How thoroughly did she present her case?

☐ Is she performing to the best of her ability, given her stage of language competency, or is she just goofing off?

With these factors in mind, you can weigh this student's performance against those of the other students in the class and give her a grade that is fair.

Conclusion

The two major assumptions we operate under when teaching the content areas are

☐ Language can effectively be learned through content.

☐ Content language provides students with both useful (in terms of knowledge) and usable language.

Time in a content-area classroom can be productive time for ESL students, even before they become as proficient in the language as their English-speaking peers. They can gain English competency by and through what they learn in class, and even though they cannot always articulate as well as their classmates, there are many alternative ways they can demonstrate their mastery of the concepts.

U.S. HISTORY   NAME _Madoka_

CHAPT 6. pages 121-124

1. Name two Indians that helped the early English settlers.

   Chief Powhatan ara Squanto

2. What was the attitude of the Indians toward land ownership?

   they had lot of cathurals

3. How were the Indians beliefs about land different from the colonists?

   the Indiane belived that the land belonged to no one: person or group

4. What is a pagan?

   or people who worshipped many gods rather than one

5. Why were the Indians destined to lose the conflict of cultures?

   because thire dieing out and poeple are mouving in to their land,

6. What was the middle passage?

   a voyage across the Atlantic Ocean

7. What were the slave codes?

   it made slaves theirowners property

8. Describe three of the slave codes?

   a. they could not vote

   b. if they run away they would be hit or whiped

   c. they could not own they things

9. Who led one of the earliest slave rebellions in the colonies?

   did Cato

10. Why was life so difficult for free blacks?

   they were not welcome into white coloial society, they had to live in a separate neighborhoods, the even had black pews in churches and they had their own black school.

RESOURCES

9

This chapter will discuss the best utilization of the resources in your school and the community. We will give suggestions about

- Coordinating with aides to use them to your—and their—best advantage
- Using buddies and tutors
- Encouraging your students' parents to participate in their children's schooling
- Using interpreters

Classroom Aides

Meeting the needs of your English-speaking students is a challenge in itself, and teachers often find themselves frustrated because they cannot give their ESL students the time and attention they need. One obvious solution to the dilemma is the use of instructional aides. The major decisions you need to make concern

- The aide's role
- Your role as teacher
- How best to coordinate efforts

HIRING AN EFFECTIVE CLASSROOM AIDE

Classroom aides and/or ESL aides are often hired in response to a sudden influx of children who speak a language that no one in the school can understand or speak. Many times these aides have no training; they are hired simply because they can speak both English and the language of the new students. In some districts the minimum requirement for hiring bilingual aides is that they can speak English. Even this criterion is sometimes difficult to meet. If you can't find a bilingual aide who is proficient in both languages, you are probably better off with an aide who is simply a good aide.

THE IDEAL AIDE
- **The ideal classroom aide would have all of the following characteristics:**

- **Good English-language skills**—not just "some" English, but proficiency in reading and writing

- **A positive attitude**

- **A working knowledge of classroom management**: how to motivate students, how to discipline, how to reinforce what you teach

- **Cultural savvy**, i.e., enough understanding of both cultures to work at ease with both

- **Patience**

An aide with all these qualities would be wonderful, but you may not be able to find someone matching this description in your district. Certainly, the decision to hire an aide should not be based solely on his or her knowledge of the ESL students' language. Good English skills are far more essential. Other useful skills would be a working knowledge of reading theory and some knowledge of the basic principles of ESL.

Although most of our discussion relates to the issue of working with paid aides, parents or bilingual volunteers may also be used in this capacity.

USING YOUR CLASSROOM AIDE

You must first decide whether the classroom aide is merely to be a clerk, or is to be given a more responsible role within the classroom. We believe that your aide is a valuable resource, and though keeping records, grading papers, and running off dittoes are all useful tasks, your aide can be used to advantage in many other areas.

Some teachers give their aide complete responsibility for their ESL students. This may be a temptation, as you have many other students to work with, but the aide, who lacks both training and experience, is *not* the teacher. Your aide should be there to complement your role, not to take over and work exclusively with the ESL students. As the teacher, *you* must be the driving force. It is up to you to be the role model, to give clear directions, to set expectations and parameters, and to use the aide to your advantage, capitalizing on his or her strengths and personality.

Your main role is to offer guidance and supervision, as well as to provide an environment conducive to rapport and open communication among you, your aide, and your students. Here are some suggestions as to how to go about it:

■ **Find out his or her strengths and weaknesses and what he or she feels most comfortable doing.** Here are some questions for the aide to answer; ask for written answers rather than verbal responses.

   ❑ What do you feel you do, or *could* do, especially well in the classroom?

   ❑ What do you feel unprepared to do in the classroom?

■ **Clarify expectations.** We suggest that both you and the aide respond in writing to the following four-part question. Provide space on the paper for four or five different thoughts.

   ❑ What do you see as each person's responsibilities in the following relationships?

   ❑ Teacher's responsibility to the teacher aide

   ❑ Teacher's responsibility to the children

   ❑ Teacher aide's responsibility to the teacher

   ❑ Teacher aide's responsibility to the children

The answers to these questions will alert you to your aide's expectations of you and to possible differences between your two sets of expectations. It will also help you define your perception of your own role and responsibilities. There is nothing as destructive to a good working relationship as two people operating under different assumptions about their roles. If these aren't spelled out and clarified at the beginning, frustration and resentment can lead to job dissatisfaction, unhappiness, or an inability to work together, which may lead to the aide resigning his or her position.

■ **Clearly define duties and responsibilities for both yourself and the aide and draw up a written contract that outlines these.** This contract can be renegotiated from time to time, and referred to during the term. In "The Aide's Role" on page 166, we give suggestions for appropriate tasks.

■ **Before school begins, meet with the aide (let's call him Mr. Chun) and help him become familiar with the classroom, the materials, and textbooks.** Make sure he also knows the jargon of the school, such as what CTBS, SAT, and so on, mean.

- Give a complete tour of the school and introduce him to the support staff of the school, the secretaries, principal, nurse, counselor, and so on.

- Introduce him to the students. Use the same title they use for you, to demonstrate that they are to treat him with the same respect. If you are known as Mrs. Burton, he will go by Mr. Chun, not Martin.

- Make sure he knows the philosophy of North American education, as well as your own personal educational philosophy. Many aides come from countries that have philosophies much different from ours. To an immigrant from Japan, for example, American classrooms can seem overly noisy and chaotic, children rude and disrespectful, and discipline non-existent.

- Make sure he has at least a basic knowledge of the principles of ESL teaching/learning. When Barb taught in a self-contained classroom, she welcomed the assistance of an ESL intern from the local university. He worked two days a week for ten weeks, participated in planning sessions, and carried on many conversations concerning learning styles and philosophies of education. But after he had left, his final report to his professor stated unequivocally that there should have been many more drills and that the teacher should have been focusing on grammar. Even after ten weeks of involvement, he was unable to accept established second-language teaching theories and continued to compare Barb's teaching methods unfavorably to those methods used when he was a student in his own country. As a result, Barb was never quite sure how much he had tried to undermine what she had been trying to do while he was working with her students—a discomfiting feeling.

- Discuss lesson plans, objectives, and the implementation of your long- and short-term goals. Make sure he knows exactly what you want him to do, either in conjunction with what you are doing in the class, or as extension and enrichment. On the facing page we include a sample lesson-plan worksheet you can use with either paid or volunteer aides.

  The "comments" section is to be used for observations and perceptions of how the day went, who did particularly well, and who had difficulty with the material. These comments are particularly useful if your time is limited, or if the aide leaves each day before you have a chance to discuss work with him. His assessment will also be useful when planning new activities.

- Make sure your aide knows the *why* as well as the *how to*. Often good ideas go awry because the aide doesn't know the reasoning behind the lesson plan. For example, if you ask an aide to do TPR

Teacher-Volunteer (or Aide) Planning Sheet

Name of volunteer (or aide) _____

Name of teacher/grade level _____

Name(s) of student(s) _____

_____

Skills to be reinforced or tasks to be completed by volunteer (or aide)

Time frame _____

Materials to be used _____

_____

_____

Location of materials _____

Procedures _____

_____

_____

_____

_____

_____

Comments of volunteer (or aide) _____

_____

_____

_____

_____

_____

(see page 142) with some students and, without understanding the principle behind it, he has the students repeat every command after him, he is defeating the purpose of TPR.

- **Ask for input.** If your aide works consistently with small groups of ESL students, he may know them better than you do and may have a clearer insight into their strengths, weaknesses, and possible reasons for behavior problems.

- **Capitalize on his strengths.** Find out if he has any special talent. For instance, Barb's aide Emma had abundant artistic talent and enjoyed making posters, wall displays, and awards for the students. Midori was a librarian and could always find a book appropriate for each child.

- **Tap his knowledge of his own culture, traditions, and values.** He has the special perspective of someone within a culture, and can bring an understanding and richness to the classroom that would be lacking otherwise. He can help you and the students understand how culture influences people's way of perceiving things, and how different behaviors result from language or cultural differences. For example, when Mary was teaching a lesson on body parts, the students were not responding as enthusiastically as she had hoped. This was suddenly made clear when her aide pointed out that she was touching them on the head and shoulders, sacred areas to Buddhists.

- **If he is comfortable with it, allow him to assume responsibility in his area of expertise.** Some aides enjoy responsibility, others prefer to be led. Still others are very conscious of what-is-aiding and what-is-teaching and will not cross that line.

THE AIDE'S ROLE

Your aide's principal role is to complement you in the classroom, to carry out your lesson plans, and supplement and enrich what you have taught. The most helpful areas are

- **Translating** (if the aide is bilingual)
  - When there is a breakdown in communication or a problem, acting as interpreter to explain or sort out the difficulty
  - Translating school notices, permission slips, and so on
  - Providing initial orientation and explaining the rules and regulations of the school and classroom to parents

- **Working in the school with individual students or in small groups**
  - Developing LEA stories (see page 94)
  - Developing reading readiness skills
  - Reading to students
  - Working on math concepts that the ESL students may not understand
  - Breaking down activities into smaller more comprehensible units for students who need extra explanation

- Coordinating with the content area teachers, previewing a lesson, then recapping it for the ESL students in their language
- Reviewing and reinforcing concepts taught to the class as a whole

- **Acting as a bridge with the community**
  - Attending parent-teacher conferences and acting as translator
  - Getting permission slips signed
  - Accompanying parents to school programs and activities to help prevent discomfort or alienation

Community Aides

Community aides, who liaise between the school and the community, play quite a different role than classroom aides. They can be a powerful force and exert much more influence on parents and community than you, so English-language skills are not as important for community aides as the ability to command respect. In many Asian neighborhoods, a man who has status as a respected member of the community is far more influential than someone whose English might be better, but who has no status. One elementary school in northern California has an older Hmong man as a volunteer. He is a clan leader, and therefore is given great respect and deference by the local Hmong population. When there is a discipline problem, Mr. Lee steps in and the problem no longer exists. He is the community liaison, interpreter, and elder, and is, by all accounts, a man to be reckoned with. His pervasive influence is invaluable to the school; he is an ally they both appreciate and depend upon.

Buddies

We discussed buddies briefly in chapter 1, "First Days"; now we would like to treat the issue in more depth.

Rather than arbitrarily assigning a "buddy" student to help out a newcomer, leaving the buddy to his own devices undirected, it is probably wise to be more systematic. One school has instituted a carefully planned and executed buddy system that has seen great success. This system, as with any successful program, has strong administrative support. It involves the careful selection and training of ESL buddies, as well as parental involvement and the use of contracts.

- Only good students who are patient, mature, tolerant of differences, and wise enough to know when to help and when to let the ESL student work on his own, are selected as buddies.

- A training workshop is given at the beginning of the year to sensitize all student-buddies to the problems of ESL students, and to help them learn ways to assist their buddies. Parents of student-buddies are given a form to sign, giving permission for their children to be buddies.

- Each buddy is matched with a student in his class and given a list of fun—and friend-making—things to do. Students sign contracts, which details things they will do with their buddies. Some suggestions include: going to McDonald's together, calling their buddy on the phone every day, inviting their buddy to their home once a week.

- Special recognition is given to buddies for their service. There is a Friendship Picnic at the end of the year, and a "Buddies Poster" (photographs of each of the buddies with their newcomer friends) is displayed in a prominent place in the school.

This program makes everyone in the school aware of the ESL students, not as a problem to be overcome, but as a special opportunity for learning and friendship. Being appointed a buddy is seen as an honor. This buddy program is a systematic, well-planned way to ease the transition of new students.

Tutors

For additional one-on-one help for students, tutors are invaluable. A tutor may be another student in the class, a more advanced ESL student, a student aide, a senior citizen, or a National Honor Society student interested in gaining service points. A tutor does not have to speak the language of the ESL student he works with. According to high school teachers Debbie Angert and Jan Booth in a conference workshop in 1987, the best candidates for peer tutors are those who

- Exhibit a willingness to help others

- Are not overly grade conscious

- Are not excessively shy

- Will be good models for appropriate behavior and good study habits

Working before or after school or during study time, they can

- Take notes during each class, giving copies to the ESL student
- Explain directions
- Clarify vocabulary
- Read the textbook material to the ESL student
- Make sure the student is following directions and working on the task at hand
- Give you feedback on his progress and problems

Parents

Contrary to the perception of many teachers, most parents are anxious and willing to help at home, and are extremely concerned about their children's success at school. The major hindrance is that they don't know *how* to help. You can help them help their children by showing them specific ways to encourage and enrich their children's learning experiences. Here are some suggestions that include the family in literacy and language learning. The title of these activities, "homefun," is important. According to Mary Lou McCloskey and Scott Enright, who developed them, homefun activities should

- Be engaging and fun
- Integrate language learning into all activities
- Necessitate both parent (or other older persons) and child participation
- Respect and utilize the family's native language
- Allow adequate time for completion
- Be presented by the teacher with preparation and follow-up
- Provide variations based on the student's language level

The most basic and important activity literate parents can do is read to their children. It doesn't matter in what language, whether their first language or English; reading in one helps reading in the other. It doesn't even have to be literature; food labels, newspapers, letters, bulletins—anything in print—will do. If parents are not literate, other family or community members can help.

HOME ACTIVITIES TO PROMOTE LITERACY

McCloskey and Enright list other activities to promote literacy and an understanding of the value and use of literature:

Record the ways family members use reading in a day

- Record examples of environmental print (street signs, bumper stickers, and so on) that students can recognize
- Collect food labels and/or containers to be used in classroom activities
- Give ESL students assignments to help them learn about their families
- Make a family tree
- Make a personal "what-happened-when" time line
- Collect funny stories about the student's childhood
- Collect family stories in a certain category—humor, superstitions, ghost stories
- Interview family members to study the history of the family
- Study a particular aspect of the parents' lives when they were children
- If parents have moved around, make a map of their migration
- Give them assignments to help learn about their culture
- Write stories about holidays and special events in their culture or homeland, such as New Year, Bon Dances, powwows, fiestas, and so on
- Write down recipes for ethnic dishes
- Illustrate traditional costumes
- Collect traditional fairy tales
- Interview others to find out traditional ways of doing things, such as how to conduct a Japanese tea ceremony
- Interview others to find out about skills they had in the homeland, such as carving, hunting
- Illustrate life as it was in their homeland
- Involve family members in projects to learn about their communities
- Sketch their rooms, their houses, their blocks
- Make a map of the student's street

❏ Make maps of routes commonly traveled, such as from home to school and to the store

Interpreters

There are times when it will be absolutely essential for you to have an interpreter—when things go wrong and you need to clarify why and how to rectify the situation; when you need to discuss with parents how their child is doing in school; when a student is sick or hurt and in need of medical attention. For these occasions, it is important that you have located and approached at least one person who is a fluent speaker of your student's language.

Interpreters are valuable assets to any teacher. If they are from the same ethnic group as your student they know the culture of the person you are trying to communicate with and can provide a bridge between your culture and theirs. They can advise you, for instance, that in their culture it is very impolite to be direct, that one communicates by beating around the bush; or that it is typical to flee from the police when you've been stopped for a violation, because people in their country are often jailed for long periods without knowing why. While the interpreter is explaining something to the student in his language, you have time to think through your next question. Most important, interpreters can verify that you and the other party are actually communicating with understanding.

The most important thing to remember when you require an interpreter is not to use children in this role. It may be all right to collar a fellow student occasionally in a casual situation, when you simply need to get a point across or understand a student's question, but for major interviews or problems, children should not be used for several reasons:

❏ Children don't have the experience, wherewithal, or training to ask appropriate questions.

❏ Using children robs adults of their authority. This is particularly true with parents from traditional patriarchal societies. Giving children such power strips them of their authority.

❏ If something goes wrong, the child will get the blame.

❏ The child may not be old enough to understand the concepts or problems you are trying to discuss, especially when they involve a medical situation.

❏ Some concepts are not directly translatable and the child may not have the cognitive maturity to explain in other words.

USING INTERPRETERS   Here are some suggestions about using interpreters, and the procedure to follow in selection and training:

- **Choose the appropriate interpreter for the situation.**

  □ Know your students and have some understanding of their cultures. For example, if you have a suicidal teenage girl, you should not use her father as the interpreter. Don't ask a Lao to translate for a Mien. Don't ask a northern industrial Vietnamese to interpret for a rural southerner. The tensions or discomfort between certain family members or cultural groups can short-circuit any efforts you make.

  □ Select someone you're comfortable with, someone who you think is reliable, who you can trust to translate your ideas accurately and not undermine what you are saying. For instance, if you are telling a student that keeping a handgun in his locker is a very serious offense, you don't want your interpreter saying, "Don't worry. I have one myself. I'll show you how to use it."

- **Meet with your interpreter before the session to talk about the situation at hand.**

  □ Explain the purposes and the goals of the meeting. You don't want to shock the interpreter with discussion of a sensitive subject when the client is already present, such as gynecological issues that he may feel extremely uncomfortable presenting, or personal issues that in his culture are inappropriate for him to broach with the other party.

  □ Make sure that he knows that he should not ask questions for you or answer questions for the student. His job is simply to interpret what both of you say; he is not your voice or theirs, but the conduit through which you both talk.

  □ Make sure that what transpires will be absolutely confidential.

  □ Make sure you know how to pronounce the names of the persons you are meeting with.

  □ Establish such basics as
    How you will be introduced
    Where you will sit, behind your desk or with the others in a circle (what is the least intimidating arrangement?)
    If it is appropriate to touch the other person
    If it is appropriate to make eye contact

If the interpreter will paraphrase or interpret word-for-word, and if he will interpret in short phrases or paragraphs

If the interpreter will give you feedback about the other party's feelings and reactions (such as telling you, "He's sad") during the meeting or afterwards

- **When the student arrives**

  - Make introductions.

  - Establish immediately that your interpreter is simply there to interpret, not level charges.

  - Look at the student, not at the interpreter.

  - Establish your student's degree of English proficiency (you don't want to be shocked or embarrassed by finding out that your student has understood many of the comments you have made to the interpreter that were not meant for the student to hear).

  - Avoid long discussions with your interpreter while the student waits.

  - Simplify your language.

  - Plan your next statement while the interpreter is relaying your message.

  - Watch nonverbal cues carefully for signs of frustration, discomfort, or anger.

- **After the session**

  - Discuss whether you solved the problem or if another meeting is required. How did the student respond to your decision?

  - Pay him. Even if it's a nominal fee, make it worth his while to have come. Schools usually have some kind of fund to pay for this, and you must compensate him for his time and effort.

Conclusion

Teachers often express their frustration at the monumental task of meeting the needs of all their students. This chapter has been written to help you tap the resources available. You're not in this alone. Using available help makes your job easier, reinforces the things you do in class, and helps you establish what you are doing right, as well what needs improvement. The main benefit you gain is support for your efforts.

CONCLUSION

Teachers in today's world juggle a complex variety of concerns. A recent chainsaw added to the teacher's juggling routine is how to effectively teach the ESL student in the mainstream classroom. If you have had little experience working with these students, you may feel overwhelmed and intimidated. You see the need to help the newcomers at the same time as trying to do a competent job of teaching your other students. Perhaps you feel that it is impossible to do both well.

First, recognize that these anxieties are rooted in your desire to do a good job. You *can* prevail, so don't let the enormity of the situation overwhelm you. Take the job in steps. Find out where your students' starting points are, and take it from there. It *is* possible to teach the ESL students and the rest of your class—and in the process all will learn from each other!

Find Support

Most important, be aware that education works best with support systems. Don't allow yourself to become so inundated with work or stress that you get overwhelmed, drained. Find support. It is almost impossible to work continually without any creative stimulus for yourself. Get input. If you live in an area that provides education workshops, sign up. Bounce ideas off other teachers, counselors, ESL specialists, or other professionals who have some experience dealing with newcomers. If you have access to education libraries, read articles and borrow books that deal with the topic of educating the ESL student. Find a confidant—someone you can share your classroom trials and triumphs with. The important point is to avoid getting walled in and burned out.

A Supportive School Program

Teachers cannot be expected to cope in isolation. According to *Thrust* magazine, a quality program depends on these factors:

- Quality staffing. This means hiring people who are trained (or willing to train) in ESL methodology and are ready and willing to work with ESL students.

- A commitment of time and personnel to training. This means encouraging and setting up in-services and allowing teachers time off to gain extra expertise for teaching ESL students.

- Money to buy materials. Publishers and resource companies are finally beginning to produce appropriate material for ESL students that take into account their various needs and backgrounds. Now money needs to be appropriated to buy these essential materials.

- A willingness to support change. Schools need to modify their priorities, their classrooms, and their strategies to accommodate the new students.

We would add a fifth factor: the willingness to modify programs as students and their needs change. For example, the Vietnamese refugees who came in the seventies were, by and large, the elite, educated professionals. The wave of Laotians and Hmongs who are now flooding many school systems are from rural villages and farms, and are largely illiterate. The Eastern Europeans who are now arriving at our doorsteps are from industrial countries similar to our own. Each type of student demands a different style of teaching and teaching methods.

A Tolerance for Gray

There are few cut-and-dried rules when dealing with language learning. If you can accept that tests may not accurately reflect your new students' knowledge and skills, that your classroom game-plan may need revision, that your ESL students may linguistically regress for no discernible reason, that there may be times when you rely on your instincts over anything else, you won't lose sleep over things outside of your control. And we suggest you keep a sense of humor handy.

The rewards of working with—and including—students with different language and cultural backgrounds are many. These students broaden the perspective of the class and contribute fresh viewpoints to your class discussions. Students unable to speak English are enrolling in our schools in ever-increasing numbers—in states such as California, one out of every six students speaks a language other than English! These students can enrich and add immeasurably to each classroom and to the lives of their classmates. We hope that this book is a beginning, a step toward making that richness a reality.

APPENDIXES

BASIC INFORMATION FOR PARENTS

To the parents of _____

The following information will help you to understand your child's new school. Please share this information with your child so that he or she will feel more comfortable at school.

If you have questions, please call _____ and we will be happy to answer them.

Date _____

IDENTIFICATION INFORMATION

Name of school _____

School address _____

School telephone _____

Name of principal _____

Name of teacher _____

Grade _____ Room number _____

OTHER INFORMATION
Schedule of school day

First bell for morning session _____   First bell for afternoon session _____

Tardy bell _____   Afternoon recess _____

Morning recess _____   Dismissal time _____

Lunch _____

Lunch options

❑ Eat hot lunch provided at school.   Cost: _____

❑ Eat sack lunch provided at school.   Cost: _____

❑ Eat sack lunch brought from home.

❑ Purchase milk only, to drink with sack lunch brought from home.   Cost: _____

❑ Return home for lunch.

Transportation options

❑ Bus   ❑ Walk

❑ Parents provide transportation

Illness   If your child is ill, please do not send him or her to school.

If your child is too ill to be able to function in class or if his or her temperature is 100° F (37.8° C) or above, we will send him or her home. (If no one is at home during school hours, please make other arrangements with the school in case your child becomes ill.)

Absence   If your child is ill or for some other reason will not be at school, please phone the school secretary or principal at _____

HOME LANGUAGE SURVEY

NOTE: This form is used for assessment and placement purposes. Obtaining this information is required by law in the U.S.A.

Date _____ School _____

Teacher _____

Dear Parents,

In order for us to help your child, we need to know the language(s) you speak at home. Please answer the following questions. Thank you for your help.

Name of student _____
                        Family name   Given name

Completed years in school _____ Age _____

Native country _____

1. Which language did your child learn when he or she first began to talk?

   _____

2. What language does your child most frequently use at home?

   _____

3. What language do you use most frequently to speak to your child?

   _____

4. What language is most often spoken by the adults at home?

   _____

_____
Signature of parent or guardian

STUDENT VOCABULARY TEST

NOTE: To be completed when new student is admitted to school. You may wish to make flashcards for this purpose using photos from magazines or catalogs. Drawings are not recommended.

Teacher _____   Student _____

School _____   Grade _____

Have student identify using English vocabulary. Use check marks to note those words the student knows. Leave others blank.

1. Colors
   - ❑ red
   - ❑ blue
   - ❑ green
   - ❑ yellow
   - ❑ orange
   - ❑ black
   - ❑ purple
   - ❑ brown
   - ❑ white

2. Numbers—Kindergarten
   - ❑ 1
   - ❑ 4
   - ❑ 7
   - ❑ 9
   - ❑ 2
   - ❑ 5
   - ❑ 8
   - ❑ 10
   - ❑ 3
   - ❑ 6

   Grades 1–3, as above plus
   - ❑ 11
   - ❑ 14
   - ❑ 17
   - ❑ 19
   - ❑ 12
   - ❑ 15
   - ❑ 18
   - ❑ 20
   - ❑ 13
   - ❑ 16

3. Shapes
   - ❑ circle
   - ❑ square
   - ❑ triangle
   - ❑ rectangle

4. Alphabet (present in random order)
   - ❑ A
   - ❑ H
   - ❑ O
   - ❑ U
   - ❑ B
   - ❑ I
   - ❑ P
   - ❑ V
   - ❑ C
   - ❑ J
   - ❑ Q
   - ❑ W
   - ❑ D
   - ❑ K
   - ❑ R
   - ❑ X
   - ❑ E
   - ❑ L
   - ❑ S
   - ❑ Y
   - ❑ F
   - ❑ M
   - ❑ T
   - ❑ Z
   - ❑ G
   - ❑ N

5. Holiday names
   - ❑ Easter
   - ❑ Halloween
   - ❑ Valentine's Day
   - ❑ Thanksgiving
   - ❑ Christmas
   - ❑ New Year's Day

6. Personal information
   - ❑ name
   - ❑ age
   - ❑ address
   - ❑ phone number

7. Body parts
   - ❏ eye
   - ❏ nose
   - ❏ cheek
   - ❏ mouth
   - ❏ neck
   - ❏ chest
   - ❏ shoulder
   - ❏ arm
   - ❏ hand
   - ❏ stomach
   - ❏ leg
   - ❏ knee
   - ❏ foot
   - ❏ finger

8. Spatial orientation
   - ❏ left
   - ❏ right
   - ❏ in front of
   - ❏ out
   - ❏ over
   - ❏ above
   - ❏ beside
   - ❏ behind
   - ❏ in
   - ❏ near
   - ❏ far

9. School vocabulary
   - ❏ recess
   - ❏ hall
   - ❏ washroom
   - ❏ auditorium
   - ❏ playground
   - ❏ locker
   - ❏ office
   - ❏ lunch
   - ❏ teacher
   - ❏ lunch room
   - ❏ principal
   - ❏ secretary
   - ❏ tardy slip
   - ❏ school
   - ❏ science
   - ❏ phys. ed.
   - ❏ math
   - ❏ school bus
   - ❏ language arts
   - ❏ drinking fountain

10. Classroom words
   - ❏ desk
   - ❏ books
   - ❏ paper
   - ❏ blackboard
   - ❏ crayons
   - ❏ notebook
   - ❏ pencil
   - ❏ glue
   - ❏ chalk
   - ❏ clock
   - ❏ eraser
   - ❏ page
   - ❏ rug
   - ❏ scissors
   - ❏ seat
   - ❏ chair
   - ❏ table
   - ❏ window
   - ❏ wastebasket

11. Clothing
   - ❏ coat
   - ❏ dress
   - ❏ jacket
   - ❏ hat
   - ❏ gym shoes
   - ❏ mittens
   - ❏ pants
   - ❏ shirt
   - ❏ shoes
   - ❏ skirt
   - ❏ socks
   - ❏ sweater

12. Safety terms
   - ❏ stop
   - ❏ go
   - ❏ walk
   - ❏ don't walk

13. Time
   - ❏ morning
   - ❏ noon
   - ❏ night
   - ❏ afternoon
   - ❏ tomorrow
   - ❏ yesterday
   - ❏ year
   - ❏ month
   - ❏ next week

14. Other vocabulary

❏ first ❏ last ❏ big ❏ little
❏ small ❏ smaller

15. Money

❏ penny ❏ nickel ❏ dime ❏ quarter
❏ cent ❏ cost ❏ dollar

16. Transportation

❏ bus ❏ car ❏ truck ❏ plane

17. Everyday directions

❏ wait ❏ sit down ❏ stand up ❏ sit on floor
❏ come here ❏ line up ❏ pick up ❏ open book
❏ touch ❏ cut out ❏ wait ❏ copy
❏ wash your hands ❏ raise your hand

18. Home words

❏ address ❏ brother ❏ sister ❏ father
❏ mother ❏ home ❏ sofa ❏ chair
❏ table ❏ bed

BASIC STUDENT INFORMATION

NOTE: This form is to be filled out at time of student's admission to school, with the assistance of parents and/or interpreter. (Health information is retained separately.)

Name of student _____

Address _____

Telephone _____ Birthdate _____ M ❏ F ❏

Father's name _____

Place of employment _____

Business telephone _____

Mother's name _____

Place of employment _____

Business telephone _____

In case of emergency, if parents cannot be reached, call

Name _____ Telephone _____

OTHER INFORMATION

Native country _____

Native language _____

Other languages spoken _____

Arrival date in U.S.A./Canada _____

Arrival date in state/province _____

Number of years in school in first language _____

Number of years in school in second language _____

Previous school enrollment in U.S.A./Canada _____

Previous English instruction before arriving in this country _____

Comes from rural/country background _____

urban/city background _____

ADDITIONAL INFORMATION

_____

_____

_____

_____

SCORING THE BOSTON CLOZE TEST

The Boston Cloze Test states that there is only one acceptable answer for each blank. This may expedite scoring the test, but we think this narrow view of test assessment may not provide the clearest picture of your students' skills. In the sample below, we combined different student answers on one form to demonstrate how to assess the answers that are appropriate, but not exact.

Once a family of ants lived on a hillside. The ants were very busy. They _____VERY_____ good care of the baby ants, _____AND_____ they stored up food for the _____BABYS_____ .

Nearby in a grassy field there _____FOOD_____ a grasshopper. He never worked. All _____TIME_____ long he played happily. When he _____PLAYE_____ the ants hard at work, he_____HAPPY_____ , "Why do you all work so _____MUCH_____ ?"

" _____BECAUSE_____ must get ready for winter when _____FIELD_____ is on the ground. We cannot _____STORED_____ food then."

ANSWERS

1. *very*—This student forgot to insert the verb, instead focusing on the phrase *good care*. Incorrect, but shows understanding.
(Boston Text recommended answer—*took*)

2. *and*—correct answer

3. *babys*—This student used the previous reference about the baby ants to fill in the blank. It is an appropriate answer, especially if the student comes from an area that doesn't require preparation for winter, or has no winter at all.
(Boston Test recommended answer—*winter*)

4. *food*—This is an example of an incorrect answer where the student probably just put something down to fill in the blank. It makes no sense on any level and is incorrect.
(Boston Cloze Test recommended answer—*lived*)

5. *time*— In an attempt to make sense of an unfamiliar idiomatic phrase, *all day long*, this student used the incorrect word. The answer is, therefore, appropriate.
(Boston Cloze Test recommended answer—*day*)

6. *playe*—This response shows an attempt for meaning at the phrase level, but it is incorrect in the context of the sentence.
(Boston Cloze Test recommended answer—*saw*)

7. *happy*—This answer makes some sense with the previous response *When he playe the ants hard at work, he happy.* It is appropriate at the phrase level, but does not make sense when read with the entire sentence.
(Boston Cloze Test recommended answer—*asked*)

8. *much*—This student used an appropriate word for the sentence; the meaning is the same as the recommended answer.
(Boston Cloze Test recommended answer—*hard*)

9. *because*—The student forgot to include the subject in the sentence, so *because* does not make sense and is therefore incorrect. However, you do gain some insight by noting the student's attempt to maintain meaning in reference to the sentence above, *Why do you all work so hard?*
(Boston Cloze Test recommended answer—*We*)

10. *field*—This answer does not make sense and is incorrect.
(Boston Cloze Test recommended answer—*snow*)

11. *stored*—Although the verb tense is incorrect, this student's answer shows he understood the concept of the sentence, thus it is an appropriate response.
(Boston Cloze Test recommended answer—*find*)

Because we looked at the types of answers the students gave, and paid no attention to such surface errors as spelling and tense, we were able to acquire more information than a simple raw score would have given us. For example, *All time long* shows that student understood that a word indicating duration belonged in that blank, even though the student was not familiar with the proper idiom. Those students whose answers were correct at the phrase level demonstrated they were making some sense of the text. (Some of those answers at the simple phrase level reflect the level of language acquisition Linda Ventriglia calls "chunking"—identifying vocabulary chunks at one time.) (1982)

If you use a cloze test for assessing your new students' skills, do not limit your results by marking your test according to some answer sheet to arrive at a score. Use the test to throw more light on how much, how little, or even *if* a student comprehends the text.

WRITING SAMPLE SCORE SHEET

SKILL AREAS	DESCRIPTION	SCORE
Content	❏ theme developed ❏ related ideas and examples supplied	**Fluent**
	❏ thought development adequate ❏ some unrelated ideas used	**Intermediate**
	❏ uneven (or no) theme development ❏ many unrelated ideas included ❏ few (or no) examples given ❏ insufficient writing for evaluation	**Beginner**
Organization	❏ good topic development ❏ opening sentence/or introductory paragraph included ❏ concluding sentence/paragraph included ❏ ideas well organized, clearly stated, and backed-up ❏ transitions included	**Fluent**
	❏ topic or opening sentence included, but no closing sentence provided ❏ weak organization ❏ inadequate back-up information provided ❏ few transitions included	**Intermediate**
	❏ no topic sentence development ❏ no opening or closing sentence included ❏ little or no organization ❏ no back-up information provided ❏ no transitions included ❏ ideas confused or unrelated ❏ insufficient writing for evaluation	**Beginner**
Vocabulary	❏ correct use of word forms (prefixes, suffixes, etc.) and idioms ❏ sophisticated word choice ❏ meaning clear	**Fluent**
	❏ generally correct use of word forms and idioms ❏ word choice correct ❏ meaning clear	**Intermediate**

	❏ many errors in word forms and idioms	**Beginner**
	❏ ineffective word choice	
	❏ words selected through direct translation	
	❏ meaning confused or obscured	
	❏ insufficient writing for evaluation	
Language skills	❏ correct use of verb tense	**Fluent**
	❏ good sentence variety and complex construction	
	❏ good control of agreement, number, word order, parts of speech	
	❏ most verb tenses correct	**Intermediate**
	❏ simple sentence construction	
	❏ errors in agreement, number, word order, parts of speech	
	❏ frequent errors in tense	**Beginner**
	❏ forced sentence constructions	
	❏ many errors in agreement, number, word order, parts of speech	
	❏ insufficient writing for evaluation	
Mechanics	❏ few errors made in spelling, punctuation, capitalization	**Fluent**
	❏ occasional errors in spelling, punctuation, capitalization	**Intermediate**
	❏ many errors in spelling, punctuation, capitalization	**Beginner**
	❏ handwriting unclear or illegible	
	❏ insufficient writing for evaluation	

INDIVIDUALIZED EDUCATIONAL PLAN

NOTE: This form is to be completed by the ESL teacher, the resource teacher, or the classroom teacher three or four weeks after the new student has been assigned to the class, or whenever an IEP is to be updated.

Student's name _____
                   Family name   Given name

Birth date _____ Age _____ M ❑ F ❑
              Mo   Day   Year

Grade level _____ Assessment test _____

Date given _____ Primary language _____

Assessment test given in primary language?   yes ❑   no ❑

SUPPLEMENTAL TESTING OBSERVATIONS

Oral production _____

_____

_____

Comprehension _____

_____

_____

Reading skills _____

_____

_____

Written skills _____

_____

_____

Summary of observed testing performance _____

_____

_____

_____

_____

_____

_____

PARTICULAR LEARNING NEEDS   Spoken language ❑   Reading ❑   Written language ❑

Other ❑ _____

Comments _____

_____

_____

_____

_____

_____

_____

_____

SHORT-RANGE GOALS   _____

_____

_____

Strategy for implementation _____

_____

_____

_____

LONG-RANGE GOALS   _____

_____

_____

_____

Strategy for implementation _____

_____

_____

_____

INDIVIDUALIZED EDUCATIONAL PLAN

NOTE: This form is to be completed by the ESL teacher, the resource teacher, or the classroom teacher three or four weeks after the new student has been assigned to the class, or whenever an IEP is to be updated.

Student's name ___Kebede_____Elsie_____
  Family name   Given name

Birth date _Jan._ _12_ _1982_ Age _9_ M ☐ F ☑
  Mo   Day   Year

Grade level ___3___ Assessment test ___LAS___

Date given _2/8/91_ Primary language _Amharic_

Assessment test given in primary language?   yes ☐   no ☑

SUPPLEMENTAL TESTING OBSERVATIONS

Oral production _Minimal response to questions._

Comprehension _Nods and demonstrates understanding of basic items. (Refer to Student Vocabulary Test.)_

Reading skills _Non-reader._

Written skills _Can write name and a few letters of the alphabet._

Summary of observed testing performance _It is difficult to determine how much effect her shyness has on Elsie's production. Observation of her classroom behavior will reveal more._

PARTICULAR LEARNING NEEDS

Spoken language ☑️   Reading ☑️   Written language ☑️

Other ☐ _____

Comments *Elsie needs help adapting to her new environment. She needs to develop skills in all language areas.*

SHORT-RANGE GOALS

To learn basic school and classroom vocabulary.
To establish the speech-print connection.
To interact with other students.

Strategy for implementation   *LEA.*
Reading aloud to Elsie.
Labeling items.

LONG-RANGE GOALS

To learn vocabulary on the Student Vocabulary Test.
To read and write simple stories.
To work in small groups on class work.

Strategy for implementation _____
Copy stories dictated to teacher.
Make one I-Can-Read book.
Do mix 'n match labels and pictures.

INDIVIDUALIZED EDUCATIONAL PLAN

NOTE: This form is to be completed by the ESL teacher, the resource teacher, or the classroom teacher three or four weeks after the new student has been assigned to the class, or whenever an IEP is to be updated.

Student's name _Keleman_ _Balint_
                    Family name   Given name

Birth date _April_ _7_ _1978_ Age _13_ M ☑ F ☐
          Mo   Day   Year

Grade level _8_ Assessment test _LAS_

Date given _10/3/91_ Primary language _Hungarian_

Assessment test given in primary language?   yes ☐   no ☑

SUPPLEMENTAL TESTING OBSERVATIONS

Oral production _Knows basic vocabulary. Accent doesn't interfere with understanding. Can communicate basic needs._

Comprehension _Can retell story taken from fourth-grade reader._

Reading skills _Literate. Transcribes report work at grade level in Hungarian._

Written skills _Simple writing, but well organized and structured. (See writing sample.)_

Summary of observed testing performance _Altho' not fluent, B. can get most of his ideas across and understands most basic conversations._

PARTICULAR LEARNING NEEDS

Spoken language ☐   Reading ☑   Written language ☑

Other ☐ _____

Comments _Balint's outgoing personality will allow him to continue to improve his spoken English. The focus will now be on reading and writing to enable him to move into the mainstream classroom._

SHORT-RANGE GOALS

To build vocabulary in content areas. To record interests and activities in daily journal.

Strategy for implementation _____

Do content work at lower level. Continue reading in primary language.

LONG-RANGE GOALS

To achieve minimum competencies in all content area classes. To mainstream and achieve assimilation into grade-level classes.

Strategy for implementation _____

Foster skills in reading and writing assignments.

INDIVIDUALIZED EDUCATIONAL PLAN

NOTE: This form is to be completed by the ESL teacher, the resource teacher, or the classroom teacher three or four weeks after the new student has been assigned to the class, or whenever an IEP is to be updated.

Student's name _Nguyen_____ _Li Trang_____
                  Family name   Given name

Birth date _March_ _29_ _1975_ Age _16_ M ☑ F ☐
          Mo   Day   Year

Grade level ____9____ Assessment test ____LAS____

Date given _3/11/91_ Primary language _Vietnamese_

Assessment test given in primary language?   yes ☐   no ☑

SUPPLEMENTAL TESTING OBSERVATIONS

Oral production _Frequently unintelligible because of pronunciation. Inaccurate grammar, halting speech, very simple vocab._

Comprehension _Knows basic vocabulary. Can retell story._

Reading skills _Knows a few words. Unable to fill in home language survey._

Written skills _Can write name. Shows limited knowledge of simple vocabulary. Syntax irregular. Many grammatical errors._

Summary of observed testing performance _At ease in interview. Li Trang's outgoing personality should accelerate his adaptation in the classroom._

PARTICULAR LEARNING NEEDS

Spoken language ☑   Reading ☑   Written language ☑

Other ☐ _____

Comments _Li needs lots of reinforcement in whole-language activities to develop his English language skills._

_____

_____

_____

_____

_____

SHORT-RANGE GOALS

To develop content vocabulary.
To build personal vocabulary.
To involve Li in group activities

Strategy for implementation _Intensive one-to-one tutoring in content areas._
Read high-interest, low-vocabulary books.

LONG-RANGE GOALS

To be able to participate in large group activities.
To turn in written assignments.
To assess minimum competencies in 3rd qtr.

Strategy for implementation _____
Work on study skills.
Begin work on personal journal project for weekly review.

INDIVIDUALIZED EDUCATIONAL PLAN

NOTE: This form is to be completed by the ESL teacher, the resource teacher, or the classroom teacher three or four weeks after the new student has been assigned to the class, or whenever an IEP is to be updated.

Student's name __Longclaws__ __Charlie__
Family name   Given name

Birth date __May 22 1985__ Age __6__ M ☑ F ☐
Mo   Day   Year

Grade level __K__ Assessment test __LAS__

Date given __9/7/91__ Primary language __Cree__

Assessment test given in primary language?   yes ☐   no ☑

SUPPLEMENTAL TESTING OBSERVATIONS

Oral production __Minimal response to questions.__

Comprehension __Difficult to know if Charlie understood as he didn't respond to questions.__

Reading skills __Not applicable.__

Written skills __Not applicable.__

Summary of observed testing performance __Charlie was extremely shy and hesitant to take tests. His abilities will need to be re-assessed as he adjusts to the environment and routine.__

PARTICULAR LEARNING NEEDS

Spoken language ☑   Reading ☐   Written language ☐

Other ☑ *pre-reading, pre-writing, sch. routine*

Comments *Charlie needs to become comfortable with the school and classroom environment. As he relaxes with the routine, he will be invited to join in the class activities to encourage his English language development.*

SHORT-RANGE GOALS

To learn school routine.
To learn twenty classroom words.
To establish the speed–print connection.

Strategy for implementation *Do coop. block work.*
LEA.
Read aloud to Charlie.

LONG-RANGE GOALS

To participate in free-play activities.
To participate in group art projects.
To participate in weekly share time.

Strategy for implementation
Copy name, key words.
Label favorite items.
Play "What's in the bag?"

GLOSSARY

BICS—Basic Interpersonal Communication Skills
The skills involved in everyday communication—listening, speaking, carrying on basic conversation, understanding speakers, and getting one's basic needs met.

CALP—Cognitive Academic Language Proficiency
The skills that are needed to succeed in the academic classroom, which include problem solving, inferring, analyzing, synthesizing, and predicting. They go beyond the BICS, demanding much greater competence in the language.

Context-reduced Language
Language that has few visual and/or aural cues to help the learner understand. This is demanding language because the learner's ability to understand the spoken or written message depends solely on his proficiency in the language. Examples of context-reduced language situations are lectures without demonstrations or visual aids; math word problems without illustrations; textbooks without charts, diagrams, or photos.

Context-embedded Language
Language that is most easily understood is embedded in a context that is rich in cues such as concrete objects, gestures, facial expressions, art, music, phys. ed., face-to-face conversations, games, hands-on activities (as with science), math computation problems, and TPR.

FES/FEP—Fully English Speaking/Fully English Proficient
Able to participate fully in regular classroom activities.

Input

The language the student hears and encounters on a daily basis. This includes directed input in the form of language lessons and ordinary conversation.

Intake

The language the student actually processes and learns, and is able to use and understand when he reads it or hears it spoken.

LEA—Language Experience Approach

A method of promoting reading in which the teacher begins with the experiences the students bring to class (or experience together), and then develops oral and written activities around these experiences. The teacher uses the students' own words to write stories, which are then used in a variety of ways.

LES/LEP—Limited English Speaking/Limited English Proficient

Understands some English, but is not fluent enough to compete academically with English-speaking peers.

Miscue analysis

A miscue is defined as the difference between the oral response of a reader and the actual words printed on the page. Miscue-analysis, developed by Kenneth and Yetta Goodman, is a method of evaluating reading comprehension using a detailed analysis of the types of errors made when reading aloud. Particular strategies are then used to help the reader correct his comprehension errors.

NES/NEP—Non-English Speaking/Non-English Proficient

Speaks little or no English.

SSR—Sustained Silent Reading

A period of time in the school day that is devoted solely to silent reading. Students read books of their own choosing. No book reports or record-keeping is required, nor are comprehension questions asked. SSR helps students develop a love of reading and increases their fluency in the language.

TPR—Total Physical Response

Introduced by James Asher, this method uses physical actions to develop language skills in second-language learners. Students are asked to respond physically to commands or directions, often in a game-like situation.

BIBLIOGRAPHY

Atwell, Nancie. *In the Middle: Writing, Reading and Learning with Adolescents*. Portsmouth, NH: Heineman, 1987.

Alatis, Penelope et al. "Learners, Teachers, and Aides/Volunteers: Bermuda Triangle or Synergy?" Paper presented at the 21st International TESOL Conference, Miami, FL, 1987.

Ammon, Paul. "Helping children learn to write in ESL: Some observations and some hypotheses." In *The Acquisition of Written Language: Response and Revision*, edited by S. W. Freedman. Norwood, NJ: Ablex Publishing, 1985.

Bliatout, Bruce et al. *Handbook for Teaching Hmong-Speaking Students*. Folsom, CA: Folsom Cordova Unified School District, Southeast Asia Community Resource Center, 1988.

Briggs, Sandra et al. *Guidelines for Working with Limited-English Proficient Students*. San Mateo, CA: San Mateo Union High School District, 1985.

Chamot, Anna Uhl and Michael O'Malley. *The Cognitive Academic Language Learning Approach*. Washington: NCBE (National Clearinghouse for Bilingual Education), 1986.

Charter, Patricia F. "Special Education/Bilingual Education: A Collaborative Model." *Thrust* (Sacramento, CA) 18, no. 6 (April 1989).

Clearinghouse on Languages and Linguistics. "Indochinese Students in U.S. Schools: A Guide for Administrators," *Language in Education: Theory and Practice* 42 (October 1981).

Cramer, Ronald. *Writing, Reading and Language Growth*. Columbus, OH: Charles E. Merrill Publishing, 1979.

Cummins, James. "The Role of Primary Language Development in Promoting Educational Success for Language Minority Students." In *Schooling and Language Minority Students: A Theoretical Framework*. Los Angeles: California State University, National Evaluation, Dissemination and Assessment Center, 1981.

Duncan, Sharon E. et al. *How to Administer the LAS*. San Rafael, CA: Linguametrics Group, 1981.

Edelsky, Carole. *Writing in a Bilingual Program: Habia Una Vez*. Norwood, NJ: Ablex Publishing, 1986.

Elley, W. and F. Mangubhai. "The Impact of Reading on Second Language Learning." *Reading Research Quarterly* 19 (1983).

Forester, Anne D. and Margaret Reinhard. *The Learners' Way*. Winnipeg, MB: Peguis Publishers, 1989.

Gadda, George, Faye Peitzman, and William Walsh. *Teaching Analytical Writing*. Los Angeles: California Academic Partnership Program, UCLA, 1988.

Gudschinsky, Sarah. *A Manual of Literacy for Preliterate Peoples*. Ukarumpa, Papua New Guinea: Summer Institute of Linguistics, 1973.

Handscombe, Jean. *When They Don't All Speak English*. Edited by Pat Rigg and Virginia Allen. Urbana, IL: NCTE (National Council of Teachers of English), 1989.

Hamayan, Elsa V. et al. *Assessment of Language Minority Students: A Handbook for Educators*. Arlington Heights, IL: Illinois Resource Center, 1985.

Judy, Stephen and Susan Judy. *The English Teacher's Handbook*. Boston: Little, Brown and Co., 1983.

McCracken, Robert and Marlene McCracken. *Reading Is Only the Tiger's Tail*. Winnipeg, MB: Peguis Publishers, 1985.

Miller, R. "The Mexican Approach to Developing Bilingual Materials and Teaching Literacy to Bilingual Students." *The Reading Teacher* (April 1982).

Ocean View School District. *Survival Guide for Teachers of NES/LES Students*. Huntington Beach, CA, 1980.

Rathmell, George. *Benchmarks in Reading*. Hayward, CA: Alemany, 1984.

Read, D. and H. Smith. "Teaching Visual Literacy Through Wordless Picture Books." *The Reading Teacher* (May 1982).

Shorey, Ravi. "Error Perception of Native Speaking and Non-Native Speaking Teachers of ESL." *English Language Teaching Journal* 40, no. 4 (October 1986).

Smith, Frank. *Reading Without Nonsense.* New York: Teachers College Press, 1985.

Trelease, Jim. *The Read-Aloud Handbook.* New York: Penguin, 1985.

Ventriglia, Linda. *Conversations of Miguel and Maria: How Children Learn a Second Language.* Reading, MA: Addison-Wesley, 1982.